Early acclaim for
The Voice for Love

"Thank you so much for your breath-taking and marvelous book! It arrived today in the late afternoon. Now it is after midnight and I can't stop reading it!" **Claudia Vermeulen, The Netherlands**

"I had my first Kundalini and Siddhi experience while reading the pages of *The Voice for Love*. As a scientist, educator, and healer, I give high regards to physical and demonstrable evidences. I feel that this book is a profound work of spirituality." **Alex H. Etemad, MD Anaheim, CA**

"*The Voice for Love* has become my inspiration, comforter, and goal—my inspiration for counseling sessions with others, my comforter when I doubt and judge myself, and my daily goal in print. I have one copy in the kitchen and one in the car to be with me everywhere I go!" **Rita Hoegel, NSW, Australia**

"I purchased your book several weeks ago. It arrived in the mail. I unwrapped it, looked at it, and thought, "Why did I ever buy this?" It sat on the bookshelf and sat on the bookshelf, until one day, I picked it up and could not put it down. It's incredible! Thank You. Thank You. Thank You!" **Wanda Anderson, Salem, WA**

"For anyone wishing to hear or strengthen their connection with that still small voice within, this book is a 'MUST READ.' DavidPaul and Candace expertly and lovingly coach the reader inward to their own endless font of knowledge and guidance. It is a beautiful, kind, gentle, and very wise book. Just the reading of it brought me to such a quiet and pea   " **Audrey Lloyd, Port Orange, Florida**

"Some of the concepts tackled so brilliantly in this book can be made to seem very complicated to us. Our egos assure us that to 'get it' will be a long and arduous task. *The Voice for Love*, in straight forward language, spells out a gentle path to helping us realize who we really are. The highlights at the end of each chapter drive home the important message this book delivers."
Jack Barney, Eugene, OR

"I had been praying to be able to hear the Holy Spirit clearly within me so I could be guided in my daily life. This book is the answer to my prayer. It is a simply written, profound, and very practical book. There are numerous exercises one can do right away to learn how to hear God's Voice, and they work! As it turns out, the Holy Spirit is not some abstract idea. He is now actually here for me as my own personal guide. Learning to hear this Voice has transformed my life!" **Annika Jisvall, Tucson, Arizona**

"I have not yet finished the book. There is so much richness on each page that I want to savor the experience, so I am going through it at a slow pace. The information contained within it is truly transformational and liberating. It is written in such a loving and supportive way and with such a positive can-do attitude that success is the only option. I look forward to continuing my journey of discovery as I wind my way through each and every page." **Linda McCabe, Canada**

"This book inspired me to connect with that Voice I knew was waiting to be invited. Using the practical exercises contained here, I heard that clear, loving voice and life has not been the same since!" **Rachael Groover, Director of Education, Neale Donald Walsh's Conversations with God Foundation**

THE VOICE FOR
LOVE

ACCESSING YOUR
INNER VOICE
TO FULFILL YOUR
LIFE'S PURPOSE

DavidPaul Doyle and Candace Doyle

THE VOICE FOR LOVE

ACCESSING YOUR INNER VOICE
TO FULFILL YOUR LIFE'S PURPOSE

DavidPaul Doyle and Candace Doyle

Published by:
HeartWise Publishing
P.O. Box 3125
Ashland, OR 97520
541-488-0426
www.thevoiceforlove.com

ISBN: 978-0-9766613-4-4
Library of Congress Control Number: 2007901889

Cover design by Gaelyn Larrick

Printed in the United States of America
9 8 7 6 5 4 3

Contents

Acknowledgements

There is a driving force within each of us to be restored to the Truth of who we are. That force inspired this book, wrote this book, and continues to bring the concepts shared in this book into the world in a variety of ways. Thank you for responding to this force within you. May the love shared in these pages help restore you to the Truth of who you are.

Preface

This book is going to take you on a journey deep within your Self, not the small self you think you are in the world, but your true Self who is limitless, eternal, and beyond your imagination. This adventure will be one of letting go, opening your mind, and playing with different ideas and ways of seeing things. At various times, you will be asked to step beyond what you think you know so that you can enter into the awareness of what is unknown, into that which cannot be described but only experienced. This book is not about teaching you a new set of beliefs, nor is it intended to be an all encompassing resource for Truth or answer all of your questions. It is designed to give you the understanding and know-how to connect with and hear *your own* Inner Voice ... that you may come to discover what is true *for you*, what is most loving and kind *for you*, and what *your* true purpose and path really are.

In discussing the Voice for Love within each of us, a variety of different words and phrases are used throughout the book to talk about this Inner Voice or Presence. Some of these include still small Voice within, Inner Teacher, Higher Self, True Self, Holy Spirit, Right-Mind, Voice for Love, and God's Voice.

Ultimately, it doesn't matter what we call this Presence within us, but it does need to be called something in order to talk about It. If you find yourself feeling uncomfortable with a specific term or phrase, be open to seeing that word or phrase in a new light. Remember, they are *just words*. You give them all the meaning they have for you. Do your best to look *beyond the words* to where the words or concepts are pointing you to, to the *personal experience* they are trying to elicit within you. If you can't get past a particular word, substitute whatever word works best for you.

Throughout the book, DavidPaul and Candace pose questions to this Inner Teacher to help build a framework for you to access your own Inner Voice. They interweave various exercises to deepen these concepts and ignite this Voice within you, and they include their personal experiences of hearing and using this Voice over the years.

Part One is designed to give you a framework for believing you are capable of accessing your Inner Voice. *Part Two* discusses the barriers to hearing your Inner Voice and provides a number of methods for overcoming these barriers. It also includes chapters on meditation and prayer and culminates with a variety of exercises for hearing this Voice within you. *Part Three* concludes the book with exercises and guidance for using your Inner Voice to discover and fulfill your purpose in life.

As you work your way through these concepts and exercises, trust what you feel in your heart, and know you are indeed being guided within, every step of the way.

How This Book Came to Be

Candace: Writing books and teaching people how to hear God's Voice within them was not something that I ever imagined myself doing. I grew up in a non-religious family. My dad was disillusioned with the Catholic Church, and my mother was agnostic. We never went to church. We didn't own a bible, and there was no mention of God. I thought Christmas and Easter were about Santa Claus and bunny rabbits, and truthfully, I didn't know anything about Jesus until I was in my 20's.

Despite this background, or perhaps because of it, I used to talk to God when I was a kid. I don't know how I knew about God, but somehow God was very real to me. I remember having lengthy discussions with God about my life, my family, and whatever was going on with me. I thanked God for the things I appreciated, and I asked for help with the things I was worried about. When I talked with God, I never wondered if God would be there or not. I never had the thought that talking to God was something that only special people could do. I never questioned my worthiness for talking with God. And sure enough, God was always there, and every encounter felt profoundly loving.

When I became a teenager, however, things started to change. Like most teenagers, I began to judge myself. I started to compare myself to others. I thought that I was bad, wrong, or somehow not good enough. Although I didn't know it at the time, I began to project that God judged me as well. I thought, "If I know how bad I am, God surely must know how bad I am!" So I began to talk with God less and less, until the dialogue ceased altogether. Eventually, I forgot about God.

When I was in my twenties, I walked into a church and heard a woman say that she talked to God as a kid. As she spoke, I remember thinking to myself, "Hey, I used to talk to God too!" The feeling of those conversations rushed back to me, and I felt the comfort and love I used to get from having them. As the flood of memories and emotion came over me, I realized that I wanted those conversations back!

In that moment, I could have said, "Hi, God, how ya doin'? Long time no talk. I've been gone for awhile, but I'm back now. How ya been?" God would have responded with ever-open arms. But by that time, I had so many beliefs about God and about myself, that it never occurred to me to simply say hello and restart the conversation. By then, I thought that talking to God was a big deal that only happened to special people. I thought one had to be very worthy to talk with God and that one had to earn that right. I also thought I had to heal my relationship with God and somehow make up for the time I was away.

So I dedicated myself to getting back into communication with God. I put tremendous effort and energy into it. I talked with people. I read books. I took workshops. One thing led to another until I found a book called *A Course in Miracles*. This beautiful book reminded me of the Truth of who I was and talked about it being God's Will that we hear His Voice. I loved this book and began doing the daily lessons.

Eventually I got to Lesson 125 in the *Course Workbook* entitled, "In Quiet I Receive God's Word Today." The lesson reads, "…. He speaks from nearer than your heart to you. His Voice is closer than your hand. His Love is everything you are and that He is; the same as you, and you the same as He. It is your voice to which you listen as He speaks to you. It is your Word He speaks. It is the Word of freedom and of peace, of unity of will and purpose, with no separation nor division in the single Mind of Father and of Son. In quiet listen to your Self today, and let Him tell you God has never left His Son, and you have never left your Self…."

I meditated on this lesson for a long time after reading it, and at some point I heard a Voice in my head say, "Surrender." Not being one who surrenders easily, I said, "No. I don't surrender to anything." A little while later, this Voice again said, "Surrender." And again, I said, "No. I'm busy meditating." Talk about missing the forest for the trees! Luckily for me, this Voice continued until finally I said, "Fine, I surrender!" And when I did, everything around me—the house, the ocean, the deck—suddenly disappeared, and the most beautiful, loving Voice filled my mind.

The Voice told me how much I was loved, how precious I was, that I had never done anything wrong. I had heard these types of things before, but hearing them within me made them feel so real. After listening to the most loving message that I had ever heard, I asked this Voice who it was. Do you know what it said?

It said it was "the Holy Spirit!"

That was *not* good news for me, and the Voice knew it. It knew I was uncomfortable with that term, so the Voice said, "No problem, you can call me God's Voice, Inner Teacher, Comforter, Guide, Constant Companion, Translator, Voice for Love or Truth ... whatever works for you. Just call me." That was 15 years ago, and I've been listening to this Voice ever since.

DavidPaul: I had a wonderful childhood. I feel fortunate that my early memories are only of playing and having fun. Though I was baptized Catholic as a young boy and attended Sunday school, Catholicism wasn't a central theme in our family. Going to church was something we did on holidays and special occasions. We were a typical middle-class family doing what everyone else did ... trying to move ahead in the world and enjoy our lives as best we could.

As I entered the ninth grade, however, my carefree existence came to a screeching halt. My parents divorced. And when they did, a fire was ignited within me for the first time in my life to become something more than I was. At 15 years of age, the highest attainment I could envision for myself was John Glenn, a celebrated astronaut and a United States Senator.

I wrote the Senator a letter asking how I could follow in his footsteps. With his suggestion that I attend the U.S. Air Force Academy, I went to the library, checked out the Academy's submission guidelines, and then charted every class, extracurricular activity, and step I would need to take to get accepted. Filled with passion and determination to accomplish this dream, I worked very hard for the next three years until I was accepted into the Academy. In the summer of 1987, ready and raring to go, I flew to Colorado Springs, Colorado to become a cadet.

I loved being at the Academy. I enjoyed the games, the challenges, the camaraderie, and the sense of purpose. As I did in high school, I planned out every move I needed to make to become who I wanted to be. Toward the end of my sophomore year, everything was going as planned, until an unexpected event happened in my life.

One month before the first day of my junior year, the day on which all cadets must sign their military commitment, I was riding in a car with two Academy friends when a Kenny G song came on the radio. About half way through the song, something unexpected happened—an explosion erupted within me, and the most profound experience of Love I ever felt suddenly came over me. It seemed as if Kenny G himself had somehow packaged up the Love within him and placed it into his music for all to receive. Filled with complete joy and wonder, a life-changing question came to mind: "If I was an old man on my deathbed, how would I have lived my life to have had absolutely no regrets?"

I immediately realized that what I wanted more than anything else in the world was to share the gift of Love that I had just received.

I then thought, "How on earth would I do that?"

Searching for an answer within me, I saw a vision in my mind of a book that impacted people's lives in a profound way all over the world. I had no idea what the book would say or how I would write it, but I knew in that moment that staying in the military was not going to take me there.

When the semester ended, I sped away on my motorcycle and never returned. Since then, my life has taken many unexpected twists and turns, and what started out as a dream to become more than I was has now transformed into a passion for being who I already am.

May you receive the Love that we have packaged up within these pages, and may this Love inspire you to live the Truth of who you are in the world.

DavidPaul Doyle and Candace Doyle
Ashland, OR
October 2003

– Part One –

Remembering
the Voice for Love

The Truth is within each of God's children.
It is a journey, rather than a destination,
that begins with a thought rather than a step.

– 1 –
The Voice for Love

*God's Voice offers that which you truly seek,
contentedness, peace, love, and the constant
reminder of who you really are.*

God loves His Child so much that He wanted His Child to always know that It is safe, It is loved, and It is whole. God created the Holy Spirit as a way to ensure that God's Child would always know these things. God gave this Voice to His Child, and this Voice is now part of that Child. It is the eternal perspective of Truth, Love, and Reality that cannot be taken from that Child. It is the Voice of God instilled within and the ever-present reminder to that Child of the Truth of Who and What it is and the Love its Father has for it.

DEMYSTIFYING YOUR INNER VOICE

DavidPaul: It seems funny to say this, but in all the years we have been listening to this Voice for Love within us, we have never once asked this Voice to explain Who or What it actually is. Our understanding of it has always been simple. We all have this Presence within us to guide and teach us in our lives, and it doesn't matter what we call It—still small Voice, Inner Wisdom, God's Voice, Voice for Love, Holy Spirit. We all have this Divine Resource within us whether we acknowledge it or not.

For years, Candace and I sat on our couch several times each week and asked this Voice questions about everything we could imagine—from how to get promoted at work, to how to best raise our daughter, make smart financial decisions, or stop fighting in our marriage—and no matter what we asked, the answers always left us feeling peaceful, hopeful, and connected with ourselves and with one another. Everything about listening to this Voice was so good that it never occurred to us to want to know more about it. Listening to it just worked.

So although it is not necessary to understand Who or What this Voice for Love within each of us actually *is* in order to access this Inner Voice or benefit from its guidance and wisdom in our lives, we felt inspired to ask the Holy Spirit this very question in order to create a foundation that we could build upon throughout the book. So here it goes:

Holy Spirit, Who or What *is* this still, small Voice within each of us?

Once upon a non-time, God, in all Its Glory, extended Itself and created a Child. Then God's Child, an aspect of God, a part of the whole, had the thought that it could do something on its own, that somehow it could be separate from the whole. In that instant, the ego was made, which is ultimately just a way of thinking that supports that part of God in believing that it is separate from the whole. That is all the ego is, and the only purpose it fulfills is the constant reminder of the illusion that that piece of God is separate from its Oneness, that there is no Oneness, and that it is on its own.

The Holy Spirit's function and purpose is to bring God's Voice to each of God's children, guiding them, directing them, loving them, and restoring their thinking to Right-Mindedness and Truth. Truth is the bridge to God—the bridge to your true Self.

As God noticed this aspect of itself holding this thought and saw the ego coming alive to reinforce that thought, God simultaneously created the Holy Spirit, not as a counter to the ego, but as a cure—to hold Truth within the mind as well, so that either would be available at any given time. There cannot be an opposite to what does not exist, but there can be a Truth to prove the inexistence of what is not, and that is the relationship of the Holy Spirit to the ego.

God, in His Perfection, is not capable of recognizing the ego and the errors in thinking that go with the ego, yet God can be aware of a need in His Child. God had the understanding that at some point that aspect of itself would tire of the thought that it is separate from the whole, and when it did, when it became so tired from that thought, it would have this inner Resource to gently guide it back to the Truth of its Oneness.

The ego has a full-time job holding the perspective that one can be separate from its Creator. The ego's full-time job is to convince you that you are on your own, roaming the world alone, and that you are never truly connected, united, or one with anything. You may be born into a family, and yet that family will come and go. You may form a marriage, and that marriage will come and go. You may have children, and they will come and go. You are never at one with anything, no matter what you do to try to attain that. That is the ego's number one job. The ego might even discourage you from having unity with your family, a true sense of union in your marriage, or a deep connection with your children to reaffirm your aloneness and your separation. The ego is diligent, hardworking, and loyal to its purpose. It will fight to the end to do its job to convince you that you are separate.

The Holy Spirit is ever patient and vigilant in its belief about your Oneness. It cannot intrude upon your dream and attempt to wake you up before your sleep is done, but it never leaves your side ... watching over you, loving you, and reassuring you that there will be a happy ending.

By creating the Holy Spirit, God provided a way to bring His Voice to each of His children as they went out into the world so that they could always remember the Truth of Who and What they are. The Holy Spirit's function and purpose is to bring God's Voice to each of God's children, guiding them, directing them, loving them, and restoring their thinking to Right-Mindedness and Truth. Truth is the bridge to God—the bridge to your True Self.

Little by little, as you hear, recognize, understand, and become aware of God's Voice in different ways—through your thinking, correcting a thought with this Voice, recognizing this Voice in another, sharing this Voice with a friend, and so on—God's Voice is brought into the world and given to each of God's children. This Voice is recognized in each of God's children and used as a reminder for God's children of the Truth so that they can overcome the world.

The Holy Spirit was given to each of God's Children by God, put within each one, and is now part of them. It is not to think that the Holy Spirit is separate from you, is really only a part of God, or will one day be separate, because in Truth, the Holy Spirit is part of you. It has now been blended and melted into you. That is why it is important to recognize this Voice for God in everyone you meet because It is part of them as well.

The Holy Spirit is within each of God's children and cannot be extracted. It is there as a constant Resource, Companion, and speaker of Truth no matter what you think you have done, what you think you are doing, or what you think you might do. This Voice for Love within you holds no judgments, never condemns, and only remembers your true Perfection. In that is the impossibility of sin or anything related to it.

It is not possible for the Holy Spirit to judge you in any way because this part of your Self can only see the Truth of who you *are* and not who you think you are. It can also see who you think you are and not believe it. It can see what you think and does not join you on that sinking ship. This Voice for God within you only knows one Truth ... and that is your Perfection, regardless of your insistence to prove otherwise. It cannot join you in any thinking about yourself other than your Perfection, though It loves you while you think insane thoughts.

When you are suffering, it is because of the belief in separation while simultaneously having the hope of Oneness. There is the hope but not the proof, and then there is fear and suffering. God's Voice is within your mind and is ever available to you to restore your thinking to Truth. In any moment you decide that you do not want to participate in the belief of separation—if you decide you want peace, if you decide you want to remember Who you are and What you are—God's Voice is there within you waiting to join with you in Truth. It has been within you since your first step into the world and offers you an alternative to pain and suffering, to fear and loathing, to vengeance and death. This Voice for Love within you, by whatever name It is called, offers you Peace, Oneness, Truth, and everlasting Life.

DavidPaul: Wow. It's funny how little I knew about this Inner Voice I've been speaking with all these years. Can you talk a little bit more about the ego?

The ego invented all of the thinking that would have you believe in the body. There is the idea that the body is the temple of the Holy Spirit—that alone may be one of the bigger misconceptions going. The body is the temple of the ego in the sense that everything that is temporary is made by the ego. Everything that is eternal is created by God. The ego is temporary. The body is temporary.

If you see another person in the world and think anything about them other than that they are a beloved and whole Child of God, then that is the ego feeding you that thought. The only Truth about the one in front of you is, "There is God's beloved and holy Child," or to put it more simply, "There I Am."

As you come across people in the world, the ego would convince you that this one is this and this one is that and the judgments go on and on and on. None of that is True. The world is made out of the thoughts of the ego. God did not make the world. The thoughts of the ego made the world. You may look upon the world and think it is a beautiful place—certain areas are beautiful, certain things are beautiful, certain people are beautiful—but if you cannot look upon the world and see that all of it is beautiful, then you are looking through the eyes of the ego.

If you look upon the world and see fear, loathing, hatred, separation, death, or destruction, these things are what the ego would convince you are happening in the world to keep you in fear and to keep you distracted from God. If you were to overcome the beliefs that you have about the body, that alone would change everything. As long as you believe that you are the body—you need the body, you are dependent upon it, you need its health, you need its well being, you need its limbs, you need its mental faculties, and so on—you are in quicksand. God's Hand is stretched out to you, but the more you struggle in your beliefs of what you have been told about the body, the deeper you sink. And God's Hand is waiting to pull you out at all times.

The ego would have you believe that there are special relationships, such as families, lovers, children, friends, and other special people in your life, though if you do not see all people as equal, then you are being deceived from seeing the Truth that everyone upon the earth is the Child of God and that you do not have a special relationship with any of them but in fact have a Union with all of them because each one of God's Children is part of your Oneness.

When each child is not received in that way, you deny yourself Oneness. Any time you act in a way that you do not like, that you do not feel is loving or kind, anytime you act in a way that is as a result of fear or control, anything that is other than understanding and accepting, it is of the ego. You may think that you are acting loving, and yet loving is unconditionally understanding and accepting. Anything other than that is acting from the thoughts of the ego.

Every time you look at your mate and want him or her to be different, judge something about them, or are annoyed at what they are doing or how they are doing it, that is the ego trying to convince you that you are separate. Those thoughts keep you from remembering that the one in front of you is a Child of God, your brother and part of your Oneness. Without that one in front of you, your Oneness is not complete. You will need the one in front of you to attain your ultimate goal of Oneness even though you have forgotten it in this moment. Without that one in front of you, the puzzle is not complete and your Oneness will never be restored. You need the one in front of you and everyone behind them to be restored as Children of God so that the Oneness may be complete. At that time the ego will cease to exist. Just as your body's survival instinct is strong, so is the ego's, for they are the same. It will fight for its life. How it does that now is to continue to convince you of your separation.

An Unexpected Dialogue

Candace: The first time I ever heard an Inner Voice, it was totally unexpected and somewhat shocking. Not because I

If you think of the ego and become afraid, that is the ego-mind working. If you become aware of the ego and you bless it and allow it to be, then you are in your Right-Mind thinking with the Holy Spirit.

heard "a Voice," but because of *what* the Voice actually said to me. I realize now that we hear what we need to hear in order to make the experience of this Inner Dialogue real to us. This is what I needed to hear to get my attention....

One Christmas, I wasn't getting along with my family so I spent the day alone at the beach. I was sitting on top of a cliff looking out over the ocean, when suddenly I realized that Christmas was Jesus's birthday. So I said hello to Jesus within myself and said, "Happy Birthday!" I then asked Jesus what he would like for his birthday and his reply nearly made me fall off the cliff.

He said, "What I would like is for you to say 'hello' to people who cut you off on the road instead of calling them 'dickhead.'"

Other than maybe my best friend, no one knew that I called people dickhead on the road. I felt embarrassed and ashamed even though there was no judgment in the communication.

Then Jesus said, "I will send people to cut you off so that they can get a special hello from you."

It was the first time that I ever had a conversation with Jesus and I knew from the dickhead comment that I really was talking with him.

For many years thereafter, whenever someone cut me off on the road, I would remember that birthday request and honor it with a kind hello. When I did this, I was able to remember that the person in front of me wasn't a problem or a nuisance, but rather another human being sharing the same path with me, at least for that moment. I felt calmer and more peaceful, and I'm sure my driving improved.

Little did I know that my first experience of hearing an Inner Voice was just a hint of what was to come.

RIGHT-MINDEDNESS

Candace: When DavidPaul and I first received the communication about Who and What this Voice for Love within us truly is, we were pretty surprised. We had never heard anything like that before, though we admit we had never asked either.

While we liked all of the insight we gained, there was one term that intrigued us—Right-Mindedness. We had heard the term before, but we didn't understand what it meant, so we decided to ask.

The mind seems to be split, and out of that split is the idea of Right-Mindedness, which is the Holy Spirit's way of thinking, and not Right-Mindedness, which is the ego's way of thinking. There is One Mind, just as there is Oneness, and it is a paradox to describe the fragmentation of this Mind because, in Truth, no one has ever nor could ever become separate from God or from the One Mind. At the same time, the belief in the ego is strong enough to convince one otherwise. So even though it is not possible, there is the illusion or the dream that separation has occurred. Within that "reality," which is not Reality in Truth but one's given reality at present time, there is "Right-Mindedness" and "not Right-Mindedness," and these are the two ways that the mind perceives or thinks.

If someone is not in their Right-Mind, they would hold thoughts of the illusion of this world—fear, separation, and death. This includes many things: the idea that someone or something is better, more valuable, or more important than another, competition, success, striving, gratification, addictions, and these types of things. These thoughts exist when one is out of their Right-Mind, pursuing distractions and illusions. They are chasing the carrot that they will never catch. This is the perfect image to describe the world—everyone is chasing a carrot on a string in front of them that they will never catch, and that is the good news. What the world has to offer, you would not want. Never catching that carrot is a blessing.

Right-Mindedness is the Holy Spirit's thinking. It is the thinking of your True Voice. It is a way of correcting your perceptions so that you are able to see yourself and the one in front of you as a Child of God. You are able to see the Truth of a situation or to understand that there has never been attack, mistake, or sin. This is not One-Mindedness, but part of the journey to One-Mindedness.

Each time you restore your mind to Right-Mindedness, you reclaim a little piece of that part of your mind for yourself and it is harder for the ego to infiltrate that area in the future, if there were such a thing. Each time you choose Right-Mindedness, each time you choose to see the Truth in a situation, you reclaim a little of your sanity for yourself. Eventually this builds and grows into a significant piece that allows you to have much more command over choosing Right-Mindedness in any given moment. You begin to know that what you are thinking, seeing, and perceiving is insane, and you would like to see differently. You stop for a moment and connect with your Right-Mind, in whatever way each one does that, and you restore yourself to sanity.

Eventually, as your mind is restored over time and this restoration builds and builds, one day what you have is Right-Mindedness. Right-Mindedness is the cure to ego. It is the correction of the ego's thinking; therefore, it must acknowledge and understand the ego in some way to be the cure. This is what will lead you into One-Mindedness, so that you never again are capable of relating to a thought with the ego. In One-Mindedness, the ego mind is gone. God does not perceive the ego because One-Mindedness perceives only the Truth.

It is easy to perceive the ego as the enemy and think that you are now perceiving with Right-Mindedness. It is important to remember that you made the ego because you wanted to have a certain experience. You wanted your autonomy, just as a teenager or young adult might decide that they are ready to leave home and be on their own and they want the opportunity to try. This is what this aspect of God has done as well. They are not wrong for wanting that. They are not wrong in how they go about it. Everything is a learning experience. Each one does the best they can to survive in the world. It is the same with these aspects of God. You made this tool, and it has done exactly what you asked of it. If you perceive the ego as the enemy, you have lost and the ego has won. Your ultimate goal is to eventually not even perceive the ego. This does not mean you ignore it, deny it, or pretend it does not exist. That is not the case at all. It is just that not perceiving the ego is the ultimate goal, and that will eventually come with One-Mindedness.

The more that one hears God, the less they hear the ego. It is just that simple. The less that one hears God, the more they hear the ego. So if you are hearing God's Voice, you are turning down the volume on the ego. They cannot talk over each other. The ego may be rambling in your mind, and you will have to stop and say, "I do not want to perceive in this way," or "I want to perceive Truth now," or "This hurts. I don't want this pain anymore." There has to be a moment where you stop the rambling of the ego and choose differently, and in that moment, you invite God to speak.

God's Voice will not speak over the ego, though it will happily speak in place of the ego. The more that you choose to hear God's Voice, the less opportunity the ego has to speak, until one day you are engaged with God's Voice when you wake up, throughout the day, and when you go to sleep. That is where you have your awareness and that is what serves your thinking, your mind, your life, and your actions. You are focused on that which truly serves you and brings you peace.

Ultimately, this continual joining with God's Voice within you offers you peace. You start to notice that peace becomes a way of life. It does not matter if there are wars going on right around you. When you notice that all you have is peace within you, it becomes obvious when that peace is threatened. You immediately notice that threat rather than living with it for years.

The more that you have peace, the more recognizable it is when you do not. You are able to quickly remind yourself that, in fact, you would like to be restored to Right-Mindedness. Then you breathe. Then you go to this Voice within you. You feel, hear, or know that connection and you breathe again. You go about your day with your peace restored, going longer and longer periods in peace, until one day, peace is all you know. That could be today or any other day you choose.

Do not think that you shouldn't bother focusing on it now because true peace is light years away. There is no such thing as time or space. No time ever transpired from the instant you had the thought that you were separate from God. You had that thought and then that thought falls away and you are restored to God, and it will be that long that you perceived that you were not with God, though in fact you never were separate.

You and the ego invented time and space to prove these theories of separation, but there is no time and no space. Start now choosing to restore your mind to Right-Mindedness, Sanity, and Truth, and know that each time you do, it builds on itself to the point that you will no longer be able to choose hearing the ego. It will not be a viable choice, not because the ego is your enemy, but because what it has to offer you will no longer see as more valuable than peace. The ego has served its purpose and now you choose peace.

When you think of the ego and become afraid, threatened or angry, you can stop for a moment, bless the ego, and thank it for all the ways that it has served you. You can say, "Until next time," and close that door and open the one to your Right-Mind. When you do this, you give yourself the gift of the kind of experience, encounter, or interaction you want to have with the ego when you do think of it. If you think of the ego and become afraid, that is the ego-mind working. If you become aware of the ego and you bless it and allow it to be, then you are in your Right-Mind thinking with the Holy Spirit. To try to never again think of the ego or be threatened by the thought that you might think of the ego, that is the ego. Give yourself the gift of peace in your thinking about the ego and then you will know you are thinking with your Right-Mind. There is nothing to fear but a thought and you can always think differently.

Part of the magic of this Voice for Love is that the more you share It, the more you have of It. The more that you give It away, see It in another, choose Its way of thinking and acknowledge this Voice in yourself, the more you have this Voice for Love in your life. That which is Eternal gains by sharing It.

Eventually, you will turn more and more of your painful thinking over to this Resource within you for restoration. You will have more and more thoughts of Truth, and there will come a time when you will hear this Voice so consistently that the ego will not have the opportunity to interrupt and

Though forgiveness couldn't be necessary or possible when one is only perceiving Truth, while one perceives with both the ego and the Holy Spirit, forgiveness is the path away from the ego—and to God.

jump in, or when you notice the ego interrupting and jumping in, it will be so obvious, so distinctly different than what you have become used to, that you will immediately be able to restore your mind to Right-Mindedness. The ego does not go away; it just becomes quiet. It is only a rambling voice in the back of your mind, so if it is quiet, it has no other power.

FORGIVENESS

DavidPaul: Where does forgiveness fit into all of this?

Forgiveness is the path of the Holy Spirit. The Holy Spirit uses forgiveness to correct perceptions and perceive Truth. The Truth of any situation is that no sin has occurred, no error accomplished, no Brother or Sister has wronged. The Truth is that the one in front of you, along with yourself, is only Perfection and cannot be, never has been, nor ever will be anything other than Perfection. When the ego begins to perceive something other than the Truth, forgiveness is the opportunity to overlook this misperception. To "overlook" means to look beyond what you perceive and see the Truth that God's Child has never done anything wrong. As you overlook the ego's perceptions, you use the Holy Spirit's thinking to go straight to the Truth.

Forgiveness is the means to quiet the ego. When one misperceives and believes what they misperceive, they believe the ego in that moment. When one looks past the misperception with the forgiveness of the Holy Spirit and sees only the Truth, they are not validating the ego or giving the ego power. They are instead quieting the ego. Forgiveness is the gift you give yourself through experiencing Truth in any situation.

Believing that forgiveness is necessary can also be a

concept of the ego, and yet true forgiveness is the opportunity to correct your thinking; therefore, forgiveness *is* the Holy Spirit's thinking and is used to restore you to the Truth. Though forgiveness couldn't be necessary or possible when one is only perceiving Truth, while one perceives with both the ego and the Holy Spirit, forgiveness is the path away from the ego—and to God.

Used in its highest form or for its highest purpose, forgiveness offers you Peace and Right-Mindedness. When used for the ego's purposes, forgiveness can take you deeper and deeper into misperceptions. One may attempt to prove the misperceptions, clarify the misperceptions, understand the misperceptions, believe the misperceptions, and then forgive the misperceptions for the sake of another, rather than for their own peace. When used by the Holy Spirit, forgiveness is the pathway to peace.

When one overlooks sin, error, or misperception, they overlook it in themselves as well as in the one in front of them. All is forgiven and only Truth is experienced. To remember the Truth of Who and What God's Child *is* gives you the experience of being God's Child. Because that is all you have ever been or ever will be, that is where your true peace lies.

CHAPTER SUMMARY

There are two thought systems in the world: one based on fear, judgment, and separation, which is the thought system of the ego; and the other based on Love, which is the thought system of the Voice for God within us.

This Inner Voice goes by many names—Voice for Love, God's Voice, Comforter, Holy Spirit, Inner Wisdom, still small Voice within—yet regardless of what word or term we use to identify It, It is a Voice or a Presence we all share within us. The purpose of this Voice is to restore our thinking to the Truth of who we *are*, to the Truth that we *are* Love, and One with our Creator. When we choose to listen to the ego's way of thinking, we choose to see ourselves and the world through the eyes of fear and judgment. When we do, we experience pain, sadness, loneliness, confusion, anger, and the other emotions associated with the ego's way of thinking. When we choose to think with our Right-Mind, with this Voice for Truth within us, we experience true peace, real love, and genuine happiness. These are the qualities of who we *are*, the qualities of *being*, and when we experience them, we know we are Home with God.

– 2 –

Our True Nature

God's Love is the Source of Who you are.
God's Love cannot change,
and neither can You.

God's Child, God's holy, beloved Child is so cherished and so loved that It is allowed to perceive Itself in any way It desires. It is allowed to experience Itself as anything, even something other than a beloved and cherished and holy Child of God. There is a saying in the world, "There, but for the grace of God, go I." In reality, it is "There, but for the perception of the ego, go I." When one perceives their Self as separate and different than the one in front of them, they can only be looking through the eyes of the ego. When one perceives the one in front of them *as their Self*, when one no longer looks with the eyes of the ego but looks instead with the Sight of the Holy Spirit, they are able to see the Truth of Who and What they *are*.

THE ONE THAT WE ARE

DavidPaul: So the ego gives us the opportunity to experience separation from God, and the Holy Spirit—the Voice for God within us— gives us the opportunity to experience the Oneness that we truly have with God, correct?

The ego's way of thinking gives God's Child the opportunity to experience what it *would* be like to be separate, while the Holy Spirit's way of thinking reminds you that you have never been separate and remain perfectly at One with your Creator.

DavidPaul: So you're saying that a separation never occurred but the ego can simulate that experience even though it's not the Truth?

Exactly, and the Voice for God within you gently guides you back to the experience of peace, joy, love, and the knowingness that you are One with all that is.

DavidPaul: I've heard you mention many times that we are One with all that is, but can you elaborate on Who we really *are*, not who we think we are in the world?

God, in all of His Love, extended that Love, which then became God's Child. God and His Child have played together, loved together, laughed together, and that has never changed. Then God's Child had the thought that it could be separate from its Creator and there was a split in the mind that then caused that Child to think it was separate. The Child then made the ego to reinforce the separation, which then fabricated the world and allowed for a place for separation to occur.

One cannot be separate from something if there is nowhere else to go, so the world was invented out of the need to go somewhere that God could not. It is like stepping into a painting on the wall and imagining now that you live in that painting and you are running in the fields and smelling the flowers and looking at the water when, in fact, you have merely projected yourself into that painting and are imagining yourself moving about in it. In Reality, you are not in that piece of canvas on the wall, just as God's Child has not left God's Lap.

When the ego and the world were made, God created the Holy Spirit as a gift to the Child to find its way out of that canvas. As the Child entered the world, the child perceived itself in fragments, in separate pieces. Now it appears there are billions of pieces of the child roaming around that canvas, interacting with different parts of itself, taking on different roles within the canvas, having a wide variety of experiences while there, and yet it is merely a projection of the Child that makes itself appear to be in all of these pieces.

Little by little, these pieces will return to the One. The first piece to do this perfectly was the one who was known as Jesus. He came into the world, fulfilled his function of remembering the Truth of Who and What he is, and restored his awareness to the One Child; however, those seven billion fragments are still in need of returning, which is only a thought away.

DavidPaul: I'm a little confused. Are we all children of God? Or is there only one Child of God?

In the world, one can be referred to as a Child of God. This is true, and yet there is only One Child of God. As you look around in the world and perceive people as good and bad, mean or kind, smart or not, and so on, you are looking at God's Child through the eyes of the ego and no Child of God is available to you with this perspective.

When you look with the Vision of the Holy Spirit, all you see is yourself in front of you, next to you, across from you,

When you look with the Vision
of the Holy Spirit, all you see is
yourself in front of you, next to you,
across from you, everywhere you look,
and you realize that you are in a hall
of mirrors and that all around
you is you.

everywhere you look, and you realize that you are in a hall of mirrors and that all around you is you. In some mirrors you look tall, in some you look short, in some you look fat, in some you look wiggly, and so on, and yet it is all you in every mirror you look in. In fact, there is only One. It just appears differently in this fragmented and distorted place.

As you step out of the hall of mirrors and look around, there is only One. That is all the world is—a hall of mirrors. You have been imagining yourself there, when in fact you never were. As each fragment returns Home to Itself, It recognizes the One Child of God that It is. The ego takes you deeper into the hall of mirrors, and God's Voice within you will guide you out.

Part of your responsibility to yourself is to take with you any other parts of you that you find in that hall of mirrors that are willing and ready to go. You do that by recognizing in a perceived other, in one that you perceive as other than you, that they *are* you, you are not separate, and that the one you imagine in front of you is God's only beloved Child. You remind the one in front of you of the Truth of who they are and you do that by being certain of who you are and you take them with you. God's Child is everywhere you look, everyone you see, everyone you like and don't like, love or don't love. When you give yourself the gift of recognizing the Truth of who you are and the Truth of who another is, it is the richest experience you can have in the world.

A TASTE OF REALITY

DavidPaul: When I left the Air Force Academy in the summer of 1989, I plunged headlong into a spiritual path. I knew I was searching for something within me, but I didn't know exactly what it was or how to find it, so I read as many books as I could get my hands on—*Illusions*, *Autobiography of Yogi*, *A*

Bridge Across Forever, the *Tao Te Ching*, the *Bhagavad-Gita*, *The Way of the Peaceful Warrior, Exploring the World of Lucid Dreaming*—whatever I could find to help me unravel this vague new purpose in life and the truth of who I was.

That fall, I applied to UC Berkeley as a transfer student. To my surprise, they rejected me, though they had previously accepted my application as a high school senior. I had excellent grades at the Academy, lived in Moscow for nine months.... It just didn't make sense. I was furious. So I re-applied, and again they rejected me.

I had only applied to two schools, UC Berkeley and UC Santa Barbara. I was accepted at UC Santa Barbara, but I wanted to go to UC Berkeley and I wasn't going to give up. I petitioned, wrote letters, introduced myself to professors, and did everything I could think of to counter their decision. In all, I received five separate rejection letters. Not willing to accept defeat, I petitioned one last time, and for whatever reason, I was accepted.

It was during my first semester at Cal that my mother suddenly passed away. She had become very sick, had a stroke while walking across the street, and was gone before I knew it. Looking back, her death was a great gift to me. Although it had only been a year since my revelation while listening to Kenny G, I was already falling back into worldly ambitions at Berkeley. So when the semester ended a few weeks after my mother passed away, I packed my camping gear, hitchhiked to Yosemite, and backpacked deep into the mountains where I lived in a cave and meditated from morning till night. It was there that I tasted for the first time in my life, the peace and joy that comes from going within.

When I came down from the mountain three weeks later, I was at peace with my mother's death and my experience of life was no longer the same. My interest in school or a successful career had vanished, and all I could think about was going within, searching for Truth, and trying to figure out my purpose in life.

When I returned to school that fall, I hardly attended my classes. Instead, I spent most of my time reading spiritual books and studying Tai Chi. Through a friend of mine, I fell into a job being a "house brother" at a sorority, receiving free room and board in exchange for watching over the house. (It was a tough job, but someone had to do it.) When I finally graduated from school the following spring, I had no motivation to get a real job or start a career, so I kept my job at the sorority house. Can you blame me?

With nothing but free time over the summer, I signed up for a meditation class at a local church. Within a couple of weeks, I was hooked. I registered for every class they offered. It was in one of these classes that I first met Candace.

This church fascinated me. They taught a way of seeing the world unlike anything else I had ever experienced. With my cushy job at the sorority house, I spent most of my time meditating and taking classes. During that time, Candace and I became close friends. Then one day, someone handed us a transcript from Jesus, channeled by Jayem. I wasn't familiar with his work, but what I read that day changed my life.

On the second page of the transcript, Jesus said, "Sin means simply to have missed the mark, to have forgotten the Truth of your being. Never once—and I know this may sound a bit radical—never once did I come into this plane to tell you that you need a savior to save you from your sins. It is not truth that I shed my blood for the salvation of many. I came with but one simple Gospel, and, unto anyone who would listen, I would look into their eyes and say but one thing: You are already the one you seek. And that which you would strive to be forgiven for has already been forgiven. And the past that has weighed you down already has been destroyed by the Light of the perfect Love that this world cannot comprehend.

"Now, I'm very sorry but I cannot come forth and give unto you forty-three years of complex techniques that if you but master them, then you might be worthy to get it. I will leave that up to many that come unto you and love to keep you guessing. And I will leave it up to those of you who insist on forty-three more years of complex struggle so you can enjoy your drama. And yet, you must in the end come to where you are even in this moment. For it is the only place that you can remember the Truth of the Kingdom: to look not with the eyes that are born of your world, but to look through the eyes of the awakened Christ....

"For many would teach you that you can create your own reality. Yet, I say unto you: your reality is one, and it is simple and it is given to you freely since before time is. You have never lost it. You have only forgotten."

In the moment that I read those words, something miraculous happened. I *experienced* the Truth of who *I am* for the first time in my life, and when I did, everything that I had ever believed in my life instantly fell away. I no longer believed any of it—what I had learned in spiritual studies, in all my years of schooling, or in my entire life—none of it. I knew that all of it was just a belief, just a thought, and had absolutely no impact on the Truth of who I am. Never before and never since has so much fallen away in a single moment. To some, this might sound frightening, but it wasn't. It was the most liberating, joyful, and profound experience of my life.

YOUR HIGHER SELF

DavidPaul: So if I am One with God, One with all that is, why use the term Holy Spirit instead of Higher Self? The term Holy Spirit makes me think of something *other* than myself.

God's Voice within you is not a word or a term. It is a Presence, a state of Being, a way of thinking that gives you the experience of Who and What you truly *are*, of what your True Nature *is*. It does not matter what words you use to describe this aspect of yourself, this quality or state of Being. It is merely to call It something so that you can put your attention on It. You can call It the Holy Spirit, God's Voice, the Voice of your true Self, the Voice for Love and Peace within you, or any other name you like.

In Truth, this Presence or state of Mind *is* your Voice, and yet who you think you are in the world is usually much less than what this Voice truly *is* and what You truly *are*. You think you are a person walking around in the world—possibly a husband, a partner, a friend, a business associate—and you become identified with these things, with these forms and concepts. It is possible to use the term *Highest Self* when thinking of this Voice within you, and yet for most people, the term Higher Self would be associated with a wiser aspect of their personality, a part within their heart or mind that is more connected with Truth or with the big picture. For some, the term Higher Self might be the voice of their own soul, and yet few would believe that they are much greater than the concept of a soul and that their true Voice is much grander than that of their soul. One still perceives them self to be separate, and for many, the highest concept that they can come up with for who they truly are is that of an individualized soul. The Truth is, you are much grander than that. You are, in fact, One with your Creator, One with All That Is, One with this Voice for God within you.

When you come to see your own Voice as the Voice for God or the Voice for Love, then indeed it does not matter what you call this Voice. Call It by any name you choose. Until then, it can be helpful to make the distinction between one's Higher Self and the Voice of your *true Self*, the Voice for God, because this distinction assists one in joining with the Self that is beyond what the mind identifies with. It helps them to connect with the deepest part of their real Self, beyond the forms, beyond the concepts, beyond what your mind can imagine, to transcend all of it and experience your true Being. That is what the Holy Spirit *is* and the Purpose it fulfills. You are Love. You are God. You are One with All That Is. And that is what this Voice for God and Love and Peace will teach you.

HEARING YOUR TRUE SELF

Candace: You said that Jesus experienced the Truth of Who He was and restored his awareness to the One Child of God. Can you tell us a little bit about Jesus's relationship to the Holy Spirit during that lifetime?

When you had the thought that you wanted your autonomy and made the ego, while God simultaneously created the Holy Spirit, there was the understanding that this was a temporary experiment and that it would have an end. That end would be when all of God's children were restored to God. Eventually, there came a time when someone stepped into the world with the hope, the dream, and the goal of hearing only the Holy Spirit and not hearing anything else. That person was Jesus.

Jesus has been referred to as God's Son, and yet every person in the world is God's Son. There is no distinction here. The only difference between Jesus and you is the desire, commitment, and follow through to hear only the Holy Spirit and to not engage with the ego. This did not happen instantaneously, spontaneously, or at birth. It happened over time, as you know it in the world, with practice and dedication and the desire to think only Truth, speak only Truth, and hear only Truth. As a result of this desire and commitment, Jesus came to hear only the Holy Spirit and came to speak only the Words of the Holy Spirit.

If you want to know what God's Voice sounds like or what Right-Mindedness is, it is the words that Jesus spoke in the

Jesus has been referred to as God's Son and yet every person in the world is God's Son. There is no distinction here. The only difference between Jesus and you is the desire, commitment, and follow through to hear only the Holy Spirit and to not engage with the ego.

world. When Jesus shared certain truths, perspectives, and Right-Mindedness, this came directly from the Holy Spirit.

It is important to note how many wanted to hear Jesus speak. People would flock to hear what he had to say. Many years after his death, people wrote down what they remember he said, and for two thousand years afterward, people continue to read those words. The power of those words comes from the Truth being brought into the world from God's Voice as spoken through Jesus. Jesus's body was used as a tool for communication and served no other purpose—that is how the Holy Spirit would use the body.

Everyone desires to hear the Truth because that is what they are. They have nearly forgotten, and yet they desire that reminder completely. When one brings God's Words into the world, many will flock to hear them. One cannot help but want to hear Truth. It is part of you. The same Voice for God exists within every child, with the same message to deliver, and every child wants that message. The staying power that Jesus has in the world comes from a single-mindedness, the single focus upon Truth and conveying only Truth. That is very attractive indeed. Jesus has not swayed for an instant since then and continues to hold only Right-Mindedness and continues to be joined in perfect clarity with the Holy Spirit. He has overcome perception altogether, so all that is left is Knowledge.

One often asks, "How can I maintain this perception of Right-Mindedness?" It would be a challenge indeed to try to fight for that perception of Reality throughout eternity. When one hears this Voice for Truth within them more and more and the ego less and less, eventually only God's Voice is heard. The ego was never real to begin with and once Reality has taken hold of the mind, all that is not real falls away. That is when True Knowledge exists rather than perception.

Jesus has True Knowledge, not a perception of Truth,

and is able to maintain that Knowledge completely and perfectly for all of eternity because that is all there is. There is no fight to attain and maintain that Knowledge. It becomes effortless because Knowledge is all there is. Jesus does not have to question or wonder about the Truth of who you are, ever, regardless of your belief that you are something other than a Child of God. Jesus does not have to waste a thought wondering if you might be right about that. He has only perfect Knowledge.

As a Child of God, having walked in the world in a body, there is the ability for Jesus to understand his brothers and sisters in the world and why they think the way they do, and just like the Holy Spirit, he does not believe what they think. One can therefore use Jesus in the same way as the Holy Spirit by asking Jesus to work with their mind to be restored to Right-Mindedness. Jesus will deny you nothing, though you must ask for it. Jesus's function is to nudge His brothers and sisters out of their sleep and to assist them in whatever ways possible in their awakening, and He does this by only seeing their Perfection.

Jesus eventually became the embodiment of the Holy Spirit and you will too. You will become the embodiment of the Voice for God, the Voice of your true Self. It is only a matter of time, and the wonderful news is that there is no such thing as time. So in an instant, having remembered the Truth of who you are and where you have come from, you too will be the embodiment of the One that is.

The only way that one can know
what is true for them is to
go within and ask. When you hear
God's Voice within you and receive
the guidance, love, compassion,
forgiveness, and acceptance that
God's Voice has for you, you will
know what is true.

CHAPTER SUMMARY

We are not the body or the personality that we experience in the world. We are not individualized spirits or souls. We are, in Truth, the One Being, the One Child, the One Spirit that *is*. We are One with our Creator; and therefore, One with All That Is. No matter what we may think or say or do in the world, we remain as God created us to *be*.

When we listen to this Voice for God within us, we are not listening to our Higher Self, we are listening to our Highest Self, our True Self, the Voice for Love within us that teaches us that we *are* Love. Regardless of what we call this Voice, it is important to distinguish what this Inner Voice *is*, so when we choose to connect with It, we know what it is we are joining with.

– 3 –

An Opportunity to Awaken

God's Love is given to me,
unending, unchanged, and unconditional,
and only a thought keeps me from It.

The world was made once upon a time, and within that time, there is life and death, joy and pain, suffering and pleasure.... though in Reality, none of those things exist. They are just part of the long dream that is the world. In that dream, anything can happen, though when one finally wakes up, they recognize that it has just been a dream, none of it was real, and everything is as it was created.

ILLUMINATING THE WORLD

Candace: You've talked about the ego and how we invented it to help us experience what it would be like to be autonomous. Can you tell us more about this and how we used the ego to invent the world?

At the time that God's Child made the ego, the ego then fabricated the world as a way to assist in your autonomy. If you live in a place where God cannot go, then your autonomy is assured. God does not go into the world because the world does not exist. There is nothing for God to go into. You believe in the world and that is how the world has come to be, but God does not. The world is a thought that you made, along with the ego that you made, to serve your desire for autonomy. It has only ever been a thought, is only now a thought, and will only ever be a thought.

There are billions of God's Children who hold the same thought. They may perceive the world a little differently—each one does—but each one has the belief that the world is real and that taking a body and stepping onto the merry-go-round that is the world is an adventure and comes with rules, goals, and aspirations. Those are all thoughts that you made. God did not create the world. God did not create the earth. God did not create bodies or anything else upon the earth. God did not create the goals or the rules or anything of the world.

As a loving parent, God does not stop His Children from thinking what they want to think. He merely loves them and waits patiently for them to think differently so that they can be rejoined with their Father completely. The world and everything in it has only the value that you give it. It has only the meaning you attach to it and the purpose you assign it. The world has no meaning for God, though God honors your need for healing your mind in the sense of recognizing that you are not and cannot be separate from God.

God did not create bodies. If one lives or dies, is healed or not, is maimed or not, that has nothing to do with God. It has only to do with one's thinking. Within the illusion of the world, the Holy Spirit uses bodies as a means of communication. That is the body's sole purpose. Of themselves, they have no other value. If a plant or an animal lives or dies, that has nothing to do with God. If the earth becomes poisoned to the point of its demise, that has nothing to do with God. God did not create it. God cannot and will not save it. It does not exist in Reality, so what is there to save?

One's worldly goals have nothing to do with Truth or God. If one pursues a degree, a position, a business, a home, a family, or anything else of the world, that has nothing to do with God and everything to do with the world, the beliefs in the world, and the need to prove autonomy. They have nothing to do with Reality or God. God created you, and as a creation of God, you are an extension of God. You couldn't be anything but Perfection. When you think of yourself as anything but Perfection, you cannot help but think of God as something imperfect. You are then implying God's imperfection by your own thoughts of imperfection. Because you are an extension of God, your Will is an extension of God's Will. Therefore, your Will and God's Will are one and the same.

The world is an opportunity to be distracted away from God or an opportunity to be reunited with God in your thinking. When you attach to the world, judge the world, or believe only what you hear and see in the world, you are taking yourself deeper into the illusion of the world. When you use all things in the world as an opportunity to connect with God, feel God, hear God's Voice, and re-affirm your Oneness with God, *all things* in the world can serve you in your awakening.

Use the world as a playground to heal and awaken yourself and your brothers and sisters rather than as a place to take seriously, to be burdened by, to fight against, to be disappointed in, or to wish were different. Allow it to be a place where your brothers and sisters are awakening with you. You can join them in getting up, stretching, yawning, and coming alive with Truth. You can join them in your heart and mind and then go out into the world to tap another on the shoulder, giving them a gentle nudge to awaken. If they fall back to sleep, let them rest a while and then move to another, nudging them gently and lovingly. Allow the world to be a place that heals. Allow it to serve you and allow what you see in the world to be gentle reminders of Truth.

ILLUSION

DavidPaul: If the world is only an illusion, does God even know when I'm talking to him?

If the world is not real and all that goes on in the world then is not real, and if God does not enter the world that is not real, God knows not what happens in the world. However, when one has a conversation with God, when one acknowledges God, appreciates God, gives thanks to God, expresses love in whatever ways they do, God hears every word. God acknowledges every loving thought and every kind intention.

When one sleepwalks about in the world ranting and raving at God, scolding God, or threatening God, God does not hear any of that because it is not His Child speaking to Him. When one is yelling at God, it is the ego that is angry; it is the ego that is yelling. Because the ego isn't real and God does not acknowledge what is not real, God cannot hear what is not real.

The angry thoughts—the ranting, raving, and threats—have never been received or heard by God. Therefore, there is no need for one to feel guilty or ashamed or embarrassed by these words or thoughts. It was not You who said them or thought them. It was not God who received them. That is how the ego thinks, how the ego perceives, how the ego reacts. It is really only the ego that hears and acknowledges its own ranting and raving. It is the ego that feels shame and guilt. It is the ego that is angry.

U se the world as a playground to heal and awaken yourself and your brothers and sisters rather than as a place to take seriously, to be burdened by, to fight against, to be disappointed in, or to wish were different. Allow it to serve you and allow what you see in the world to be gentle reminders of Truth.

Given that, all that is left is forgiveness and peace, knowing that your relationship with God is completely intact, as it always has been and always will be, regardless of what you think you may have thought or said or done.

DavidPaul: I'm afraid people are going to flip out when they read this and throw the book into the garbage. Can you make the concept that the world is only an illusion a little more palatable?

For the most part, people identify with what they see with their eyes, what they hear with their ears, and with the thoughts they think in the world. But the Truth is, you are so much greater than what you see, what you hear, and what you think. You are the changeless extension of God, and you remain as God created you to be. So no matter what you think you are or what you think you see and hear in the world, those things are not the truth about you. They are merely thoughts projected from the mind that would try to convince you that that is who and what you are. That is the illusion we refer to. You are not those *things*. You are the Essence, the Spirit, and the Being from which those things arise—the thoughts of the world, the thoughts within the mind, the thoughts that you think you see and hear—those are merely projections from the mind, and when one identifies with those projections, they cannot simultaneously identify with their Source, with their true Nature, with the state of Being from which all thoughts arise and exist within.

Part of this teaching is to help you focus your attention upon that which is eternal, formless, changeless … that which is pure Being, so that you can come to identify that Source and that Presence as your Self … so you can pull your identity out of the things in the world and return it to who you truly *are*. When you make this transition from not just thinking you are Spirit, but to *experiencing* with all of your Being that you *are* Spirit, you will then project that Truth, that state of Mind, that Love onto all things in the world.

Just as the mind projects thoughts of separation onto the world and you identify with those projections, when you have come to identify with Who you truly *are* (and you project only Truth upon the world), then all things in the world will be seen for what they *are* ... that there is only God, that God is all that *is*, and that you only see your true Self in everything you perceive because you *are* all that *is*.

When one is thinking with the thought system of the ego, one projects that thought system upon one's Self and perceives only separation. When one identifies with the thought system of the Holy Spirit and projects that thought system upon them Self, one sees their true Self in all things, as all things, as the Source of all things. So it is important to let go of the illusion that you see before you in its myriad shapes and forms so you can restore your attention and focus to the Truth of Who you are. Once you do, you will look out upon the world with the Vision of the Holy Spirit and see illusion no more. You will see that only Love is Real, only God exists, and that you are One with all of It.

Be patient in this process. Be patient with yourself as you come to heal this split within the mind ... that you can come to see things from a unified perspective, from a place of Wholeness and Oneness. The more you focus on this Voice for Love within you, the more you will come to see this Love as your Self.

✦ Exercise – Using the World to Awaken

It is easy to hear that God did not create the world and then think that the world has no meaning for you, or to hear that God is not in the world, therefore, the world must not have any value. The world is what you made. It can be used to either assist you in falling deeper into your sleep, or, with the help of your Inner Voice, assist you in waking up.

Take some time to walk about in the world—whether that is in your home, outdoors, at your work, or wherever it may be—and as you walk, simply notice what you notice. Do not try to notice something, but allow something to become known to you. Imagine for yourself how what you notice could assist you in reminding you of the Truth of who you are and/or reminding you of the Truth of God.

Everything you made has the potential to either take you further away or bring you closer to the Truth, depending on your perspective. The ego's perspective will take you away, and the Holy Spirit's perspective will bring you to the Truth. In allowing yourself to focus on something and becoming aware of how it can assist you in remembering the Truth of who you are and the Truth of God, you allow the world to serve you in the most amazing ways and ultimately quicken your journey Home. You may want to spend a few minutes or longer every day practicing moving about in the world with this intention and noticing how everything has the possibility to serve you with the right state of mind.

For example, when you pay for something at a store or receive a bill in the mail, you might have the thought that money is the root of all evil. You might have the thought that you never have enough money. You might have the thought that things are too expensive ... or you can have the thought that you have this resource to get what you need and that, for the most part, you always have had it and always will. You can stop for a moment and give thanks for always having what you need in the world, knowing and trusting that will always be the case. You can also go beyond that and allow the money to be a symbol for you that you always have what you *truly* want and need, which is God, God's Love, and God's Voice. In terms of Right-Mindedness, you can go as far as you want. Right-Mindedness can be a small shift into a positive perspective or a deeper shift into a place of gratitude or connection with God, possibly transcending the world and allowing something to restore you to the Truth.

It can be the same for a dead animal in the road. One might think, "Oh, that is awful," or "I hate death," or something about the person who hit the animal or the animal itself .... or one might stop and give thanks for having had that animal in the world. One might take a moment to trust that it must be perfect.... "This animal's life must be complete. It must have fulfilled its purpose." Or you can go further and take a moment to connect with God ... to remember and to trust that, in Reality, there is no death. Spirit cannot be killed. The body is temporary, transitory, and illusory, and that the essence of whatever it is that appears to have died has never changed and will never change.

Everything in the world, with a certain perspective and a certain intention, can be used to bring you closer to the Truth. It is only to stop for a moment and to notice your thoughts, which habitually gravitate toward the struggles of the world, and to acknowledge them, thank the ego for doing its job, and to search within your heart and mind for that which is really True, for that which gives you true Peace, Joy or Comfort, because everything in the world can serve you in that way if you allow it.

IN THE WORLD, BUT NOT OF IT

DavidPaul: A few weeks after the life changing experience Candace and I had reading the channeled transcript from Jesus, we went to Stinson Beach to play. We spent the day enjoying the sunshine, throwing Frisbees, and splashing around at the water's edge. At the beach, Candace told me that a lifelong dream of hers was to swim in the ocean. Having grown up in

E verything that you made has the potential to either take you further away or bring you closer to the Truth, depending on your perspective. The ego's perspective will take you away, and the Holy Spirit's perspective will bring you to the Truth.

Northern California, she had always been frustrated with the temperature of the water. I too had always loved the ocean and wanted to live in a place where I could comfortably enjoy it.

While playing, our Frisbee accidentally landed on a man lying in the sun. When we went to retrieve it, he told us that his name was Matisha, and he asked if he could join us. We noticed that he was reading a book called *A Course in Miracles*, and we asked him about it. He told us that he taught people in prison about the Truth of Who they *are* using that book and that he was on his way to Hawaii in just a few days to do some teaching. He said that he spent every winter in Hawaii, swimming in the ocean, connecting with dolphins, and enjoying the warmth and sunshine. As he described his lifestyle in Hawaii, our eyes lit up! Candace and I turned to one another at the same moment and smiled from ear to ear. Somehow, we just knew we were moving to Hawaii!

The following weeks were a whirlwind saying goodbye to friends and family, quitting my job, and getting rid of my belongings. Before I knew it, I was stepping off the plane on Kauai carrying only a backpack. The day I arrived, a terrible rainstorm struck. Torrential downpours flooded the island for nearly two weeks. Tired of sleeping in a wet tent, I rented a studio apartment on the North Shore. Two days later, I fell into a part-time job at the Princeville Hotel. By the time Candace arrived only one week later, I had already begun a life on Kauai. With plans in place to visit a friend on the Big Island, Candace soon continued onward and eventually settled down in a small town overlooking Kealakekua Bay and her beloved dolphins. It seems ironic that we never ended up living on the same island together, but at the time, it never occurred to either of us to turn our friendship into something more.

When I stepped off the plane on Kauai, I was overflowing with life. I had never felt so incredibly free. For about three months, I lived in a state of constant bliss and joy without a care in the world. I truly felt enlightened. I don't remember a single ego thought passing through my mind.

And then it happened. I noticed a stray thought of fear pass through my mind one day as I drove to work ... and then a judgment ... and then another. Somehow, like a machine, the ego had suddenly been turned back on within my mind.

Afraid of what was happening, I became hell-bent on not loosing the profound state of peace and joy that I had gained. Not knowing what else to do, I began to watch my thoughts like a hawk. If I noticed any ego thought arise within my mind, I would swiftly strike it down. I would block it. Crush it. Make it go away. I became a thought destroying machine and proud of it. Nothing was going to take me away from living the Truth of who I am again, I though! But I was mistaken.

As the months slowly passed, the light and life within me grew dimmer and dimmer. I was still absolutely certain of the Truth I experienced only months before, but no matter how certain I was of its Reality, I did not have the understanding or experience to apply this Truth to my life. As a result, I slowly began to disconnect from myself and the world one thought at a time. I had no idea that I was subtly, ever so subtly, judging everything that passed through my mind as I proceeded to eradicate each thought one by one.

With each passing day, I grew more and more apathetic, depressed, and lifeless. Not understanding that I was literally rejecting the world and everything in it by trying to eliminate my thoughts in this way, I soon found myself meditating from morning till night because it was the only thing I could do to find any real peace or joy. It was the only time in my awareness that I could truly lay down my sword.

After many months of sitting in silence, unable to find or acknowledge any value in the world, I summoned my determination to be done with this meaningless game of life once and for all. If meditation was the only place I could find peace, I thought, I had to take it to the end. I couldn't take the life I had made any longer. My depression and apathy were just too overwhelming to live with. So I went to a deserted beach one day, sat down beneath a tall tree, and vowed to remain there until I became enlightened. It seemed to be the only way out.

I meditated under the tree for nearly ten hours straight, but as the sun dipped below the horizon that evening, a deep realization came over me that no matter how badly I wanted to escape the lifeless world I was living in, I wasn't going to be able to will myself out of the world and into enlightenment. I just knew it wasn't going to happen for me. So I opened my eyes, got up, and humbly walked home.

This experience became a tremendous turning point for me in learning how to live a life filled with Truth while still walking in the illusion of the world.

CHAPTER SUMMARY

The world is a collection of thoughts that arises out of the thought system of the ego to assist us in experiencing what it would be like to be autonomous, to be separate from our Creator. When we attach to or believe the thoughts of the world, we come to identify ourselves with these thoughts and forget the Truth of Who we really are.

As we focus our attention on the Voice for Love within us and allow this Voice to remind us of what is True, we begin to pull our energy, our attention, and our identity out of the thoughts of the world and restore them to our true Self. When we do, instead of projecting the thought system of the ego onto All That Is, we project the thought system of the Voice for Love onto All That Is, until eventually, we come to see that the illusion of separation was never real to begin with and we remain exactly as God created us to be.

– 4 –

That Which Is

God knows only Perfect Love.
God sees only Perfect Love.
God is only Perfect Love.

God is the All Loving, All Knowing Creator of what *is*. God's Love knows no bounds. God's Love is limitless and enduring, and God has nothing but Love to be, to share, and to do. God's Love is all there is, all there ever has been, and all there ever will be. When one sees something other than God's Love, they are just mis-seeing. It is not possible for there to be anything else. When you see anything other than God's Love, you can shake your head and look again knowing that you must be mistaken. God's Love is the source of all that is. When one looks through the eyes of Love, that will be all they see.

THE ESSENCE OF LIFE

Candace: Because our beliefs about God impact us in so many ways, can you talk to us about Who or What God truly is?

It is easy to say that God is all there is. To understand this, you would have to understand the distinction between what is Real and what is imagined ... what God created and what you dreamed. In Reality, God is all there is and only God and what God created exist. God, God's Child, and God's Voice are what exist, and God's Child and God's Voice exist within God.

God just is, and God can only be what you project Him to be. The beliefs of God being love or peace or truth are worldly concepts. It's the highest attainable in the world, and yet once you step out of the illusion of the world, you see that those are not what is the most attainable for God. God just is. There are no stories, no concepts of good or bad, right or wrong, peace or not peace, love or not love. God just is, without any expectations, without any demands, and without any judgments. The highest concept of what that might look like in the world is unconditional Love.

God is unconditionally loving because God is nothing else. God is only capable of seeing you as Perfection. You are not capable of being anything other than Perfection, except in your own mind. Because God loves you the way He does, you are free to pursue your own dreams. These have nothing to do with the dreams of the world, though your dreams have brought about those dreams as well.

Candace: What then is God's Will for us?

God's Will is that you be restored in your thinking to the Truth of who and what you are. Because you are an extension of God, your Will and God's Will are the same. Your Will is

God is unconditionally loving because God is nothing else. God is only capable of seeing you as Perfection. You are not capable of being anything other than Perfection, except in your own mind.

One. It cannot be different or separate. Your Will then is to restore your mind to your Oneness with your Father, and that includes your brothers and sisters. Your Will and God's Will are the same.

It is not God's Will that is directing you in the world. God's Will is directing you out of the world. Generally speaking, it is the ego that is directing you in the world. In its fight for your autonomy, the ego is doing its job and fulfilling its function as you asked of it.

There is the expression, "Oops! I created a monster." One may have had the intention to make a wonderful thing, some useful and meaningful thing, and without realizing the full ramifications of what they were making, they innocently made a monster. In a sense, that has been how the ego has served you. The ego has fulfilled its purpose and function by giving you the gift of autonomy. Then there came a time when you said, "Thank you. I am done with this gift." And the ego said, "I am not." That is when the pain and suffering began and compounded to the point of needing to acknowledge it and do something about it.

That is the beauty of making a monster. As in this case, there is the incredible motivation to overcome the ego and fight for your return to God. Before the monster was experienced, there was the idea that one option would be to return Home. As the monster has become more prevalent, the desire for Oneness drives God's children Home. It establishes a force that motivates God's children with so much power that it assists them in overcoming the world.

God waits patiently right where you left Him, with open arms and a loving heart, eagerly awaiting your return, and nothing you can do or will do could ever change that.

Levels of Truth

DavidPaul: There are so many truths floating around in the world. What's the difference between truth with a lower case t and Truth with a capital T?

There appear to be several different levels of truth. God's Truth is the original Truth, as It was created and can't be changed, ever, under any circumstances. God's Truth is the one true Truth, and that would be the ultimate Truth that's true for everyone and that most people cannot see right now. This Truth allows there to be no right or wrong, good or bad, better or worse, only what is.

God has never judged. God has no needs. God hasn't wanted anything. God hasn't expected anything. God just is and the Truths that go along with that are the simple Truths about your constant Perfection. You have never been anything other than Perfection, regardless of what you think you may have done in the world. You have never done anything wrong. You have never been separate. You are God's perfect Child.

Then there are truths that are part of the illusion, what might be true for one or true for many. These are based primarily on perception rather than the true Truth of God. There are universal truths, "Do unto others" and things like that, which are not God truths. They are concepts that help you have less to forgive yourself for, and again, forgiveness is not a God concept. There are many things that might be considered universal truth. They might come from a higher place than other types of truths and yet, they're not true in God's Mind.

It is not a God truth that there is no time and space because in God's Reality there is no time or space. That is only man's reality. So man has to fabricate the truth that there is no time or space because man invented time and space. God doesn't have as a universal truth that there is no time and space because it simply doesn't exist. It doesn't need to even be addressed. You can have what's true for you. You can have your beliefs about God. You can have your beliefs about the world and about yourself, and those would be truths for you. Some of them may seem to be higher truths, and yet rarely would they be God Truths.

When you begin to let down the wall that you have built between you and God and begin to join with God, so much of what you thought was truth falls away because it is only truth as perceived in the world, not Truth as perceived in God. If God is all there is and you have never strayed from God, it is hard to understand what could possibly be True in the world ... perhaps only your ability to have long and vivid dreams.

CHAPTER SUMMARY

God just is. The highest concept we can project onto God is that God is Love. No matter what we think or say or do in the world, we remain as God created us to be.

A majority of the spiritual concepts that we have come to believe are true in the world are merely stepping stones for us in coming to experience the Reality that, like God, we simply *are*.

It is God's Will that we be restored to the experience of Truth. Because our Will and God's Will are One, it is our true desire to be restored to the experience of Truth as well.

When you begin to let down
the wall that you have built
between you and God and begin to
join with God, so much of what you
thought was truth falls away because
it is only truth as perceived in the
world, not Truth as perceived in God.

– Part Two –

Hearing the
Voice for Love

God's Children are the messengers
of His Message to each other.

– 5 –

Hearing Your Inner Voice

God's Voice rings True in the world through every Brother and Sister upon the earth.

God's Voice is the Gift that God gave to each of His children as they stepped into the world. Hearing God's Voice is your most natural ability and it serves you unconditionally. God's Voice has one purpose and that is to restore you to the Truth of Who you are, and It will do that in whatever ways you seek.

Because there are only two voices to listen to, it becomes very easy to know when you are hearing God and when you are not. The challenge comes when you are not hearing this Voice and you want to choose differently, as well as hearing this Voice and applying what It says to your life. You can use this Voice to help you learn how to recognize It, how to choose It, and how to live It.

HEARING AN INNER VOICE

Candace: Hearing an Inner Voice can mean different things to different people. Can You share Your perspective on what it means to hear God's Voice within us?

Hearing God's Voice can be hearing the wind blow by, hearing music, hearing birds flying overhead, a car horn, or someone saying "thank you" or "I love you," and it can also be hearing specific words that come from within your mind and heart … that come from inside of you.

The Holy Spirit is the Translator for God and acts as the Voice for God. It communicates to you and through you using God's Voice, God's Mind, and your Mind … providing comfort, guidance, direction, and love when you ask for it. This communication is something that isn't offered unless it is asked for. This Presence is within you at all times and yet cannot give you guidance, comfort, or direction unless you have sought it.

You may not have consciously said, "God, please guide and direct me," but you have, on some level, invited that guidance or direction in, and then you will hear It. It could be what you might sense as intuition, an inner voice, some kind of conscience, some way that you know to turn left instead of right, or to not go to this particular place at this time. You are receiving guidance whether you consciously asked for it or not.

You can hear God's Voice at any time under any circumstances. For many people, they find it easier to hear this Voice when it's quiet, perhaps sitting down in a meditative or reflective state without a lot of distractions. Yet that might not be the time that you need to hear the words the most. It may be that you are standing there with the world falling down around you and there is chaos, mayhem, and hysteria everywhere you look and you want to hear guidance and comfort and Truth. While the world is crumbling down around you, you can go within and ask the Holy Spirit to join with you and communicate with you.

As a daily practice it might be that you sit quietly, go within, and seek communication without distraction so that you can be comfortable with what it is you are connecting with, how you are doing that, and the Voice that you hear, so that you know it is the Voice for God, and you know they are God's Words coming to you. You then have the opportunity to redevelop your faith and to reconnect with yourself and with God so that in a time of crisis you have confidence that what you are connecting with is, in fact, God's Voice.

Say, for example, that the world is crumbling down around you. You might stand there and ask for Truth so that you can be reminded and reassured that there is no such thing as death. You might ask for a perception of Truth that gives you peace as all of the chaos is carrying on around you, and you can know that you are just watching an exciting movie and you need not be in fear. Or you might stand there with the world crumbling down around you and say, "Where do I run to be safe?" You might be guided left or right or up or down to a safe physical place, as if there were such a thing.

God's Voice will join you where you are. It will not say there is no such thing as "safe" if that's what you are seeking, because this Voice will give you what you are seeking, which of course has nothing to do with deceiving you. If there is a "safe place" for your body as the world crumbles down around you, you will be guided to that place. If you say instead, "I would rather have peace in this moment than fear," this Voice within you will guide you to that as well. You may have the illusion that your fear is alleviated through the thought of a safe place to take cover, and yet that is temporary peace ... though if that is what you seek, that is what you will be given. This is one of the wonderful things about the Holy Spirit. It

The Holy Spirit is the Translator for God and acts as the Voice for God. It communicates to you and through you using God's Voice, God's Mind, and your Mind ... providing comfort, guidance, direction, and love when you ask for it.

will join with you where you are rather than expect you to be somewhere else.

As you stand there seeking peace while the world is crumbling, by joining with God, joining with this Presence of Love within you, seeking that which is Real, you will be delivered from your fear, delivered from your perceptions of fatality and destruction, and you will be brought into God's Arms, onto God's Lap, and held and rocked and comforted. Your body may still be standing in all of the chaos and mayhem, and yet the body is what you made, not what God created. In Reality, it does not exist.

Candace: I've heard that I need a translator to hear God. I've always felt like I've spoken with God directly. It's hard to accept the idea that I need a middle man. Why does one need a translator, and is it possible to hear God directly?

If one had no more barriers to Truth within them, they could hear God directly. That is a very big IF. When one no longer hears the ego and only hears the Holy Spirit, that is when the door becomes open to connect with God directly. At this point, with the ego so prevalent in the mind of God's Child, there needs to be a Translator, one who understands the ego and one who understands God, and the Holy Spirit fulfills this function perfectly.

There are no barriers to Truth within the Holy Spirit, and the Holy Spirit can hear God directly. While those in the world have barriers to Truth, which are simply thoughts and beliefs, it is not possible to hear God directly. When one thinks they are hearing God, they are hearing God's Voice and that is in effect the same as hearing God. It is just not hearing God directly. God is speaking to you and God is communicating with you through the Holy Spirit or Right-Mind. So yes, you are hearing God. God is talking to you personally, and this is done through the Translator. Once those barriers are gone, the Translator will still exist, though It will no longer have that purpose. You will join with God directly.

Candace: I've had the thought that the Holy Spirit translates between people as well. Is that true?

Yes it is. Most think that the Holy Spirit is the Translator for God in the sense of God being this big booming Presence in Heaven whose Voice is projected into the world and the Holy Spirit translates, and yet because everyone *is* a Child of God and has this Translator within them, the Holy Spirit can be used as a Translator for the one in front of you as well as for God.

If you are having a conversation with someone, the Holy Spirit can translate for you what they are saying so that you hear their words as the language of Love, the language of Right-Mindedness, the language of God. You do not hear what appears to be coming from their physical body regarding the world. You hear, instead, Love.

You can hear this Voice within your mind translating God's Words to you so that you can speak God's Words into the world and share these Words with the one in front of you, and at the same time, you can hear God's Words in the one in front of you with that Translator in your Right-Mind. It is the same Voice that is in the one in front of you and all the other ones upon the earth, so it is God's Voice in the one in front of you or within you that allows the words to be translated, either as they leave their lips or as they reach your ears.

The gift of this Translation is heavenly indeed, and it is just like learning any new language. At first, it is difficult to understand. You may not understand any of it. Then you are able to pick out words and pieces. Over time, you are able to understand much of what is being said, and eventually you are able to speak that language to another. The words come more freely and are better understood and received. The more you practice that language and live with that language, the more it becomes your own. Soon, there comes a time when it is so natural to speak in that language that you do not have to think first and you find yourself speaking it to one who does not know it, because it has become such a natural expression.

Whether you have a knack for languages or not, this one is your true first language. Once you begin to hear it and understand it, it will come back to you, and it will be easier and more natural to you than whatever language you have been speaking in the world. Love is your first true language.

Surrender

Candace: Six weeks after DavidPaul and I decided to move to Hawaii, I landed on the Big Island. After settling into my new home overlooking Kealakekua Bay, I spent every morning swimming with the dolphins and would then go home and do my daily lesson from *A Course in Miracles* and meditate on the lanai for hours. While so much of the Course rang true to me, I struggled with the idea that one could not talk to God directly. The Course teaches that the Holy Spirit is the Voice for God, the go-between, the Translator, and that as long as we live in the world, we need the Holy Spirit to communicate with God. I didn't like this concept because I believed that I had been talking with God all my life.

One day I was doing Course lesson 125, which was "In quiet I receive God's Word today." It starts like this:

> "Let this day be a day of stillness and of quiet listening. Your Father wills you hear His Word today. He calls to you from deep within your mind where He abides. Hear Him today. No peace is possible until

His Word is heard around the world; until your mind, in quiet listening, accepts the message that the world must hear to usher in the quiet time of peace.... He has not waited until you return your mind to Him to give His Word to you. He has not hid Himself from you, while you have wandered off a little while from Him. He does not cherish the illusions which you hold about yourself.... Today He speaks to you. His Voice awaits your silence, for His Word can not be heard until your mind is quiet for a while and meaningless desires have been stilled. Await His Word in quiet."

So I did. And in the quiet of meditation I heard, "Surrender." I was not one to surrender, especially if I did not understand who I was surrendering to, so in my mind, I said, "No." A few minutes later that Voice said, "Surrender." Again I resisted. This continued for a while until finally, and I do not know how or why, I surrendered.

When I did, it was as if a valve had opened and water came rushing in, flooding the space. The Voice flooded my mind, and I heard the most beautiful and loving communication about myself that I had ever heard before, and I knew that everything I heard was true even though I had never thought those things about myself. I asked this Voice who It was, and It told me that It was the Holy Spirit, which was the Voice for God. It was "the Voice" in lesson 125 that would share with me the Word of God.

During this experience, the only thing I was aware of was this Voice. There was nothing else. The lanai was gone. The ocean was gone. It was such a tremendous feeling; I felt full and loved and at peace, while also thinking that I might explode. It seemed that I had felt this feeling before, though I didn't know when or where. I just knew I wanted more of it. I knew that it was true.

If one had no more barriers to Truth within them, they could hear God directly.... At this point, with the ego so prevalent in the mind of God's Child, there needs to be a Translator, one who understands the ego and one who understands God, and the Holy Spirit fulfills this function perfectly.

Then the Voice guided me to think of my best friend, and as I did, all this amazing communication came into my mind about her. We had been best friends for a number of years, and yet these were things I had never noticed or thought about her, and they were all incredibly loving and true. Hearing these things about her allowed me to see her differently, and for the first time, I had the experience of really loving her unconditionally. A little while later, my housemate came home and I had the thought of him, and again, my mind was filled with communication about him. It was incredibly loving and very true, and I had never noticed those things about him either or seen him in that light.

Whenever my thoughts drifted off to other things, the Voice pulled me back to It. I continued to hear this Loving Presence throughout the day and continued to be amazed by all of the communication I received and all of the things I became aware of. It was as if I had a friend sitting in my mind talking to me and making loving observations wherever we went. These conversations felt so comfortable and natural, as though I had just reconnected with a long lost friend.

Later that day, I called DavidPaul and told him about my morning. I said, "You will never believe what happened to me!" He said, "Yes, I will," and listened patiently to the whole story. He was very excited and could feel that it was true. He called me back a few days later and told me that he was going to have a friend call, and he wanted me to give her communication from the Holy Spirit! He had been guided, without realizing it, to push me to share this Voice with others.

Needless to say, I was terrified at the thought of sharing this Voice, but for some reason, I agreed to share It with her. We set up a time for her to call when we would both be free for an hour. While I was meditating before she called, I was guided to say a prayer of intention for our time together. The prayer that came to me as I waited was, "May it be with your blessings, God, that these words that come through are Yours and only Yours. May they bring joy and light to those who hear them and wisdom and knowledge to those who don't. Amen."

When this woman called, we spoke for a few minutes and then I told her that I would connect with the Holy Spirit and begin the session. I was very afraid and certain that I would have nothing to share with her, but since she was already on the phone, I had to proceed.

I said the prayer that I had been given and then I asked this Voice if It was willing to come through me. I heard, "Of course, precious one." I prayed to get out of the way, and then I began to see words form in front of my closed eyes. I read the words out loud as they slowly appeared in front of me. It was both nerve-racking and exciting at the same time. Forty minutes quickly passed and the woman on the other end of the line was very happy, validated, and filled with a sense of peace about her life and her situation.

When we hung up, I jumped up and down and danced around the room. I was so excited that I was able to share God's Voice with her and so grateful to be able to hear Truth. One thing I noticed was that the words I shared with her were also applicable to me. Even though her situation was different than mine, the message of Truth and the perspective of Peace worked in my life as well. The words that I shared changed the way I saw the world and the people in it. It was as if this Voice for Truth within me was speaking to us both at the same time, exactly where we were in our lives.

THE EVOLUTION OF TRUTH

DavidPaul: I don't understand why there are so many different versions of truth out there when supposedly we are all hearing the same Voice within us. Why is it that we each hear something different from "The Voice for God" when we go within and ask for guidance or communication?

For the most part, when someone asks a question, they are looking for an answer that they can actually understand ... an answer that makes sense to them, that they can take in and do something with. If someone asks you what 2 + 2 is and you answer with anything other than 4, you are most likely giving too much information, complicating the matter, and not talking to the person where they are. They have not asked, "What is the meaning of 2 + 2?" They have not asked why 2 + 2 equals a particular number or anything else. They have just asked, "What is 2 + 2?"

When you ask a question of God, to present an answer other than what you have asked would not be of Truth. If you ask, "What is the meaning of life?" or "Why am I here?" there are at least seven billion answers to those questions. The answer could be one thing on Monday and something different on Tuesday and something different next year because what you are asking for will be given to you and what you are truly asking at any given time can change.

When you ask God's Voice within you a question, you will get Truth every time. You will get as much Truth as you are truly asking for. You will get as much Truth as you can understand, take in, absorb, make sense of, work with, utilize, apply, and no more. What would be the point of receiving more? It would be wasted and it could perhaps confuse any other Truth that might have otherwise been understood.

If you were to say to God, "I want to receive communication that is above where I am right now. I want to receive the highest Truth," you would not know if you were receiving the highest Truth because you would not be able to understand the Truth in the message. When Jesus delivered the Sermon on the Mount, much Truth was shared on that day, and everyone heard something a little different depending on where they were. So the highest Truth might be told, and you will take from it what you can and nothing more. You cannot take more

When you ask God's Voice within you a question, you will get Truth every time. You will get as much Truth as you are truly asking for. You will get as much Truth as you can understand, take in, absorb, make sense of, work with, utilize, apply, and no more.

from it than you can understand. You may be given the highest Truth every time you connect with this Voice within you, and what you can take from that is as much as you can understand in that moment.

This Voice for Truth within you does not judge what you seek, nor does It have an agenda for how you receive or interpret that which is given you. God's Voice knows the Truth about you, no matter what seems to be happening in the world. God's Voice always recognizes the perfection of your evolution, the perfection of your understanding, the perfection of your expression of God. It does not question whether you are sharing Truth or not. It knows that only Truth exists and can only see the Truth in all things.

✧ EXERCISE – FOCUSING ON KINDNESS

When one looks around in the world, more often than not, one notices pain and suffering, crime and punishment, anger and resentment, selfishness and inconsideration. These are the things that make the news and as such, they are what one puts their attention on or becomes aware of. The habit in the world is to notice these things when, in fact, most of what is occurring in the world is kindness and cooperation, love and appreciation, courtesy and gratitude, care and respect.

As you go out into the world today, make note of all the ways you notice people being cooperative. Notice how many people do kind and courteous, thoughtful and caring deeds throughout the course of the day ... whether it is holding open a door, greeting someone with a smile or a kind look, or perhaps allowing another person to go ahead of them in a line.

You might discover that you take for granted everyone who shows up at work each day to serve you—the cashier, the gas station attendant, the doctor, or the mechanic. You may not realize how loving or kind it is for everyone to stop at a red light so you can go through the intersection safely. Notice how much love and consideration is actually going on around you.

It is easy to see the person sitting on the sidewalk asking for help and then focus on the problems of the world, such as homelessness and suffering, and to not notice the people who give this person money, food, or a kind word. The opportunity for those people to give is a tremendous gift, and the one who is asking is offering that gift.

As you go about your life in the world today, notice all of the kindness, courtesy, and cooperation and focus on how much of that is occurring. Rather than the 1 in 50 times that someone is rude to another, focus on the 49 out of 50 encounters where people are kind, respectful, or courteous. Focus on that which is of Right-Mindedness, Love, and Truth, and remember that even when you see that 1 out of 50, or 1 out of 100, or 1 out of 500 encounters that might seem unkind, remember that it is just a cry for help.

YOUR OWN DIRECT CONNECTION

DavidPaul: Some people might perceive hearing God's Voice as a form of "channeling," but after many years of hearing this Voice within us, that is not our experience. To help explain the difference between channeling and hearing God's Voice, we asked the Holy Spirit for clarification.

All of the definitions overlap here and there, but what is important is that you hear Truth, seek Truth, follow Truth, and move in the direction of Truth. God's Voice has been instilled within each person to be a Translator between that person and God. God is this giant mass, and within God are you and everyone else. You are part of God. God's Voice is part of you.

You cannot "channel" the Holy Spirit because It is part of you and within you. There is nothing to channel. You are simply tuning in to a particular frequency of your Self and communicating that frequency just as you would change stations on a radio.

God's Voice is within you and you are within God.

God put the Translator right inside of you where you could not lose It and gave you full and complete access to It. This Translator is a direct line to God, and It is there for you to hear in a way that you won't hear other things. You cannot "channel" the Holy Spirit because It is part of you and within you. There is nothing to channel. You are simply tuning in to a particular frequency of your Self and communicating that frequency just as you would change stations on a radio.

In asking about other speakers of Truth, there are many who can either hear the Holy Spirit themselves or who have a grasp on Truth and share It. If this works for you, that is great. What you are looking for ultimately is your own direct communication. For those who hear God in their own way, that is wonderful. For those who do not, the Holy Spirit is there for them as God's Translator. Then if you add more translators to that, in particular ones that are not literally installed within you, you are getting a less quality translation. The Holy Spirit is a direct translator that is part of you. Your own unique, direct connection to God is already there within you. Using a different one will not quite be the same. Use what works for you, and all of the things one uses along the way are steps toward that end. It is the seeking that matters, not necessarily the end result.

If you were to get a sign that gives you the direction you've been asking about—if you hear something, if you read something, if someone tells you something and you have the sense that it is a message meant for you—it doesn't matter where it seems to come from. You have a knowing within you that this is a message and to take heed. Whether it be from God, the Holy Spirit, or your Right-Mind, it is a way of serving you, guiding and directing you—perhaps hitting you over the head, perhaps doing what it takes because you've been seeking and haven't noticed the answers. You continue to seek and the answers continue to elude you, when, in fact, they've been there all along. These "forces for good" will conspire to move you along in the direction that you seek. It is irrelevant or inconsequential who or how or what, just that the Universe would give you that which you are seeking. It simply operates that way.

Continue to seek Truth. Continue to seek Right-Mindedness, God-Mind, that which can truly serve you in your heart and mind, and know that you will ultimately have that which you seek. How you get there is irrelevant.

REGARDLESS OF ONE'S FAITH, RELIGION, OR PERSONAL BELIEFS

DavidPaul: What about people of different faiths or belief systems, or people who have entirely different religions? What about those who run from hearing the term "Holy Spirit," or who don't believe in God? Are they hearing the same "Voice for God" as well?

Regardless of one's faith or whom one believes in, whenever one hears Truth, they are communicating with the Holy Spirit. Whoever you think you are praying to, with, for, or about, there is only one true Creator, which, in this form, we are calling God. You may call God whatever you prefer.

For those who have heard this Voice and have asked It its name, they have brought the recognition of the Holy Spirit, by that name, into the world. Once in the world, any name is as good as another, and yet the Creator has called this Voice the Holy Spirit and has given It to everyone equally.

Within the world, all of God's children have the opportunity to pursue whatever path, belief, religion, god, and/or faith they desire, and yet behind every opportunity is the same Source. Behind every one is the Reality that all of this is a dream, and the illusion that is the world does not exist. Know that regardless of what you call "Source," everything you hear that is True, everything you hear that is Right-Minded, loving, or kind comes from God through God's Voice or Interpreter by whatever name It is called. It matters not *what* It is called, just that It is called.

Chapter Summary

Hearing God's Voice does not only mean hearing an actual voice in your head. In the broader sense, it means connecting with the Presence of Love, Truth, and Peace within us and within all things, regardless of the form It takes. It does not matter what we call this Voice or Presence. It does not matter what we believe about God or what belief systems we hold in the world. Every time we join with this Presence of Love, we are "hearing God's Voice."

Hearing God's Voice is different for everyone. We each hear this Voice in our own ways, and *what* we hear is based upon what we are truly seeking. Because we are perfect expressions of God, whatever insight, understanding, or communication we receive in any given moment is perfect, and *what* we receive from moment to moment can change as our understanding and experience of Truth evolves and deepens.

This Voice for God is within you. It is the Voice of your true Self, and you will hear your Self in whatever ways are perfect for you in this moment.

– 6 –

The Benefits to Hearing Your Inner Voice

When we look through eyes of Love,
we see a world of Love beaming back at us.

When one begins to really hear their Inner Voice and begins to listen in such a way as to benefit from what they are hearing, the gifts of this experience are indescribable. Hearing and not hearing is the difference between sleeping and being truly awake, quite literally. When one is not hearing this Voice, they are sleepwalking through their life. As one begins to hear and to listen, they begin to come alive, and the Truth of who and what they are begins to direct their life in such a way as to truly live.

It is easy to follow the path of least resistance when you are sleepwalking, yet when you are awake, alive, moving, and really being pulled Home, your life takes on meaning, purpose, and satisfaction in ways you have never even dreamed of. As you live a life based on Truth, you recognize who you are, you recognize who the one in front of you is, and you understand why you are here, where you are going, what is Real, and what has just been a dream. Only Peace and Love and Joy exist within that, and despite how you may have been living up to now, that is truly all you seek.

GAINING YOUR SELF

Candace: While driving in the car one day, DavidPaul and I decided to brainstorm on all of the benefits we had received in the past 15 years from hearing God's Voice within us. We wrote down over 60 different benefits ... from healing painful experiences and having more peace and joy in our lives, to understanding the meaning of life and why things happen the way they do. While we could probably write an entire book on the benefits to accessing this Inner Voice, we thought we would start by hearing what the Holy Spirit has to say about it first:

Even though God's children live in the world and have forgotten their Oneness with God, there is still an inkling left within each child that causes them to have a tiny bit of the memory that they are One with God. Even with all of the thoughts and beliefs they have acquired that have caused them to think they are unworthy, God isn't real, they are fine on their own, or other beliefs that keep them from remembering fully—despite all of that—there is still a glimmering within them that they are One with God. Somewhere deep down, they remember that God is their true Creator and Source Whom they yearn to return Home to.

For some, the journey seems impossibly long even though it is just a thought away. For others, it seems that their Oneness with God was only a transition (that was then and this is now) and they have moved on from God. There are more than seven billion thoughts that would keep one from God, and yet this tiny spark of remembrance of Oneness keeps one thinking about God, keeps one trying to understand God, coming up with belief systems around God that work for them and make God real. There is a pull within each of God's Children toward this end, and with the opportunity to hear God, one can remember Truth.

The words, the perspective, and the love that comes through God's Voice are a reassurance and a promise for that restoration to one day be complete. You are the only one keeping you from it. You are already perfect, worthy, and fully and completely loved by God; you just have to eventually remember that. Whether you remember in this instant, or this instant, or this instant, it doesn't matter. In each instant that you remember, you are born. The idea of one being born again and again and again in each moment that you remember your Oneness with God is the true definition of being "born again." You are born in Reality, not the world.

Truly, one gains everything by hearing God because there is no Reality in the world. When one hears God, they are in Reality for that moment. When one hears God, they experience validation or proof of what they have always known somewhere in the back of their mind, no matter how buried that knowing may be beneath the accumulated thoughts and beliefs that say otherwise. Hearing God proves to the little spark of hope that was there all along that there is more to life than what meets the eye.

It is so easy to live in the world, to attempt to succeed and excel in school, to succeed and excel in work, and to make the perfect family, home, and lifestyle. "Lifestyle" here means the right place to live, the right home, furnishings, car, clothing, vacations, or entertainment system. One goes about continuing to accomplish, attain, succeed, and excel in all of these worldly ways until they die. And so many people

What does one gain from hearing God? They gain themselves. They gain God. They gain everything that really is, everything that really matters, and with that, all the peace and comfort they can experience.

walk around in the world saying, "Isn't there more to life than this?"

This is just a game that one plays for fun, for learning, and for different experiences. This is not reality. When one can hear God, they can step out of the need to strive, excel, and succeed, and instead seek peace and love in their hearts, in their minds, in their lives, in their relationships, and in the world so that the life they are living is an expression of God and a remembering of the Oneness that you are with God. This allows you to live a life that has meaning in the moments, encounters, and experiences rather than in the things.

It is not that one must sit and worship God in a church, a God that looks like this and thinks like that. When one talks about false idols, they are talking about the belief that striving to own the perfect entertainment system is more important than striving toward expressing kindness toward their family. Many people put much more energy and resources into creating the perfect entertainment system than they do into showing their family that they love them. Some think they are showing their family that they love them by buying them the right entertainment system. When one has learned that joy or happiness comes from a screen and they experience love when they watch a story on that screen, then it makes sense that the perfect entertainment system is a wonderful way to love one's family.

Ultimately, what each one seeks from the bottom of their hearts is God's Love, true Love, the remembrance of their Oneness, the remembrance that God is everything, God is good, and they are within God always, safe and sound, loved and cherished, accepted and understood just as they are. To sit with God with this perspective is so much more fulfilling and rewarding than anything that is on the screen.

What does one gain from hearing God? They gain themselves. They gain God. They gain everything that really *is*, everything that really matters, and with that, all the peace and comfort that they can experience.

SHARING YOUR INNER VOICE WITH OTHERS

Candace: Hearing and sharing this Voice within me that first day over the phone was so powerful and rewarding that it seemed to open a door within me to share this Loving Presence with others. DavidPaul continued to send people to me to share this Voice with, and others soon found me as well. Early on, I made a commitment to never offer or suggest that someone receive communication, but somehow, if someone was meant to have it, the subject would come up. There were times when I was in line at the grocery store or hanging out at the beach, and strangers would start talking to me about wanting to connect with God, feeling disconnected from Source, or needing more divine guidance and direction in their lives. At those times, I would tell people about hearing this Voice, and each one would ask for a session. I knew these people were sent to me from God, and I was grateful to be sharing God's Voice with them.

I also made a commitment to always say yes to anyone who asked to hear this Voice. I encountered many people who wanted guidance on how to access their own Inner Voice, and our time together was focused on that. Sometimes, I worked with people who just wanted answers to their problems. This was frustrating for me because I really wanted to help others hear this Loving Presence within them rather than solve their problems. I wanted to "teach a man to fish," rather than catch a fish for him every day.

Over time, hearing this Voice became a regular part of my life. I often sat with friends on the beach or took breaks on a hike and we would tune in to this Voice. On many of those occasions, Jesus or Mother Mary would come through me instead of the Holy Spirit. They would introduce themselves and communicate specific things related to those personalities.

In a way, I preferred this because I was still uncomfortable with the term Holy Spirit and Who and What that Voice truly was. I found that many people were unfamiliar with the Holy Spirit by that name, yet they had a deep affinity for Mary or Jesus. Eventually, as I became more comfortable with the Holy Spirit, Jesus and Mary stopped coming through me.

At that time in my life, I came to realize that my job was to share the Holy Spirit by that name and to help others become comfortable with God's Voice in this form. One way to do that was to write a book about hearing the Holy Spirit. Writing a book wasn't my idea, but I tuned in to the Voice every morning and wrote down what I heard. One morning I was given a book title, *Planting a Garden within Your Heart and Mind to Sow God's Seeds of Love* (this would be a manual for hearing God's Voice in all that you do). Not knowing the first thing about how to write a book, I continued to write down the guidance I received and waited for more direction.

A little over a year after I first started hearing God's Voice in this way, DavidPaul was feeling very frustrated because he really wanted to hear this Voice as well, so I was guided to start holding "playshops," which were fun workshops. During those gatherings, I shared this Voice with the group and answered people's questions. Afterward, we did different activities designed to spark this Voice within them and helped them recognize what they might already be hearing.

I found that many people experienced hearing a "voice," but they had trouble discerning whose voice it was or trusting the integrity of the message. We practiced using God's Voice and testing and trusting our intuition so we could strengthen our ability to be guided. Many people had sought a tangible connection with God, and by doing the exercises in the playshops, they had been able to ascribe certain experiences, signs, and guidance as coming from God. It was very exciting!

GUIDANCE AND DIRECTION

The opportunity to experience God, hear God's Words, and receive Truth as guidance and direction is like finding a map when you are in a million acre forest and have no idea where you are or how to get out. You suddenly stumble upon a map, figure out how to read it, orient yourself, find the trail, and then very efficiently, directly, and smoothly find your way home. It is the same with this Voice. All one needs is the guidance and the direction to restore their mind to Truth, which puts them right in their Oneness with God.

Candace: Hearing this Voice within me has been so incredibly fulfilling that it's hard to imagine living my life without it. Over the years, DavidPaul and I have sought guidance and insight from this Voice on life altering decisions as well as the most mundane topics imaginable. These questions have ranged from how to write a wedding ceremony and prepare for having a child, to when to sell stock, how to "sleep train" our daughter, or which vitamin and mineral supplements to take, if any. God does not have an agenda for what we seek guidance and help with. God's Voice will join us wherever we are—from how to deal with PMS to understanding the Universe.

The story of how DavidPaul and I became a couple is a wonderful example of how we have received guidance in our lives. After living in Hawaii for several years, I woke up one morning with the realization that I wanted to be married and have children. This was a surprise to me, as well as to my live-in boyfriend. Though we loved each other and planned to be married "in the future," as it turned out, the future was something that was never going to come.

While I was wondering what to do about this dilemma, a friend needed a house sitter for a few weeks, so I moved out to clear my mind and seek guidance and direction. Though I was listening to this Voice for Love within me, it was hard to

With the opportunity to experience God, to hear God's Words, and to receive Truth as guidance and direction, it is like finding a map when you are out in a million acre forest and have no idea where you are or how to get out.

trust that what I heard was true because I didn't like what I heard—that my boyfriend was not my life partner.

I called DavidPaul to tell him where he could reach me for the next few weeks. The next day he called to tell me that he had been in love with me for some time and wanted to make a life with me. I had sensed this at some point, but the reality of it was quite a surprise. He was 6 years younger than me, and I had always considered him my little brother. We were very close, on very similar paths, and we shared a lot of love between us, but marriage and family seemed impossible.

Confused and unsure, I asked this Voice for guidance and direction, but because I thought I knew what was best for me, I continued to doubt what I heard. I was then guided to watch for signs and let them direct my path instead.

Immediately, one of my jobs ended and another slowed to a crawl. My living situation changed and my boyfriend decided definitively that he could not commit to marriage and children. I then had a run of massage clients from Silicon Valley, where DavidPaul had moved to, who all told me what a wonderful place it was.

DavidPaul offered to send me a round-trip airplane ticket so I could visit him, and I agreed. What he ended up sending me was a one-way ticket ... with the understanding that I could return to the island any time I wanted. When I inquired about putting my things into storage, however, there were no storage units available on the island.

As this momentum built, I received the following communication:

Greetings and blessings to you precious one. Indeed this is a special day. We haven't communicated in this way (writing in my journal) in some time. How are you? We've missed you.

Your life is a funny one right now. I hope you are not taking it seriously. Of course you are supposed to see DavidPaul. He was sent to you a long time ago. Remember? He is a gift to you for all of your hard work—and vice verse. It is possible that you could make something work with each other. How badly do you want it? God's Will is one thing, but it is your desire that brings about all that you have in your life. First is the desire, then the goal, then the attainment of the goal.

Due to free will, God cannot intend for your path to be something other than what you want. It is only that many have forgotten what it is they asked for before they came here to Earth, and God is a reminder about that intention. God reminds you of the path you planned for yourself before you arrived in the body.

God's Will is that you be happy. Not at the expense of others, but for the benefit of others. If you have something that would make you so happy and also be of benefit to others, of course that would be God's Will for you. It is not His Will that you suffer, remember? It is only your belief in suffering and the need for it that would bring that about in your life. You have already learned all there is to know about suffering. This is a lifetime of joy, play, celebration, rejoicing ... and that is what the two of you will do together. Of course, there will be difficult times, times where there is discord, confusions, hurts, resentments, but no more than there is now for DavidPaul while he is alone and not benefiting from the opportunity to join with another. And no more than there is for you in the relationship you are completing, yet without the same opportunities for joy.

It is essential that you both be vulnerable, open, honest, sweet, loving, innocent, and as little children in this process because then God can work through you to show you how to be with each other. You have never been with anyone like the other and it will be different indeed. God bless you both in this journey and know of course that We are with you always, loving you, guiding you, laughing with you, and showing you the way.

Blessings. Amen.

Candace: The signs and communication continued like this until finally I knew that I was supposed to leave paradise and move to California to explore the possibility of a life with DavidPaul. Despite that I planned on never leaving Hawaii, with the guidance and the signs that I received from this Inner Voice, I didn't doubt my decision and I never looked back.

UNDERSTANDING

DavidPaul: In addition to all of the peace, love, and guidance we have received over the years from hearing this Voice, another wonderful gift has been the opportunity to learn and grow in our understanding of Truth. A small but eye-opening example of this unfolded while I was writing the following paragraph for this book.

I originally wrote: "We have had a yearning in our hearts for a long time to share the Words of the Holy Spirit with others. Even though God sees only our Perfection and does not validate the illusion of separation that we have made in our minds, He is joyful when we open up to receiving the love that He has for us, when we hear His Voice, and create a fulfilling relationship with Him. He wants to communicate with us. We have known in our hearts for a long time that sharing this Voice and supporting others in hearing this Voice within them was our service this lifetime."

After writing this, something just didn't feel right about it, so instead of trying to figure it out on my own, I decided to go within and ask. This is what I heard.

All projection. It's not possible for God to be joyful or not based on what you do. God is joyful, period. It may help you to be joyful when you connect with God in that way or when you connect with you, but it is not possible to do something that would make God happy. That's one of the paradoxes in

Wherever you are, whatever you're doing, whatever you're thinking, whatever you believe, God just loves you. God hasn't gone anywhere and neither have you. There are just a few beliefs and thoughts between you and God. That's all.

relationship with God. So many people live their lives wanting and trying and yearning and striving toward doing that which would make God happy. There are entire religions devoted to it, masses of people aspiring to that end, and yet there is nothing that anyone could do or not do that could make God happy or unhappy. God just is, and God is not the effect of you. You can put in your statement, "God is happy, and it seems that we are happy when we do these things," and that would be the point. God already is happy and doesn't need to do anything to become happier.

DavidPaul: So God doesn't have any desire for us to hear His Voice?

Ultimately, no.

DavidPaul: So why did He give us the Holy Spirit?

For you, not for Him. For His Children who have gone on their way so that they can find their way back Home. That has nothing to do with God being happy or not happy.

DavidPaul: So God doesn't even *want* us to find our way home?

God doesn't have an agenda for you to find your way Home. God is not going to be happy or unhappy because of what you do. That doesn't necessarily mean that God wouldn't want you to be rejoined with God in your thinking. God loves you in the way that can allow you to be where you are because God loves what is. Why would God want for something? God has no agenda for His Children because God understands that they have never been separate. God understands that they have never strayed, only in their minds. What could God want for them when they're already perfect and they're already One with Him? There is nothing more to want for His Children.

Even to say that God wants your happiness is a projection. You want your happiness. You think that may come from a connection with God, so it is projected onto God, "God wants my happiness and that can be achieved through a connection between the two of us. And God will be happy if there is a connection between the two of us." However, in Reality, God just loves you. Wherever you are, whatever you're doing, whatever you're thinking, whatever you believe, God just loves you. God hasn't gone anywhere and neither have you. There are just a few beliefs and thoughts between you and God. That's all.

God is everything and you are part of God, and because you judge certain things about yourself, certain parts of you, you have the idea that God can judge you as well, as a part of Him. But this doesn't happen. There are no expectations, no hopes, no dreams, no goals, or agendas for God's Children. All of God's Children have free will to go out into the world or not, seek their fortunes or not, pursue their dreams or not, and God does not have the idea, one way or the other, that this is right or wrong.

God simply watches what you do and looks through eyes of Love and understands why you do what you do, so there is no need for you to do something else. If you are happy, that's fine. If you are not happy, that's fine. That has nothing to do with God. It is your choice in every moment to perceive God or not, experience God or not, acknowledge God or not. It is your choice in every moment to be happy or not ... to live in the world or to live in Truth. Reality is just one thought away.

DavidPaul: For me, this was a perspective about God that I had never heard before. It is also a perfect example of how Candace and I have come to learn all that we have from this Voice. We simply ask questions when things come up, and this

Voice within us answers them in such a way that takes us a little deeper in our understanding each time we ask.

✧ EXERCISE – DISCOVERING WHAT IS

Take a few minutes to contemplate God. After doing so, make a list of all the things that you think God is and then keep writing until you cannot think of anything else that God is. For example:

1. God is all powerful.
2. God is loving.
3. God is vengeful.
4. God is real (or God is unreal).
5. And so on....

The list could be a hundred items long if that is what occurs to you about what God is. Then go over your list and notice in what ways *you are* the things that you wrote down.

God is all powerful — In what ways are *you* all powerful? In Truth, you are the maker of the world. You are all powerful in creating your reality. God does not create it for you.

God is vengeful — In what ways or at what times are *you* vengeful? Maybe it is just a thought that you want someone to get what they deserve, or this type of thing. But even if it is "just a thought," that is equally as powerful as an action.

In what ways are you loving? In what ways are you real or unreal? Begin to notice that everything you believe about God is really what you believe about yourself, at least sometimes, or in certain situations, or in your thinking.

When you have finished going over your list, imagine for a moment that God does not have ego and does not think with the Holy Spirit. God is just Truth, and from the highest worldly perception imaginable, God is Love. Begin to notice for yourself the Truth of Who God might be, rather than who you think God is.

Uncovering What Really Matters to You

What people truly seek is a way to live their lives so that moment to moment, hour to hour, day to day, and year to year, they are happy, fulfilled, contented, and at peace with themselves, their mind, their life, and the world. Applying this Voice to your life is what will give you that. No pill, no program, no book, no religion, other than your own true religion, will give you that. By making the commitment to hear God's Voice within you and in deciding to hear God's Voice through whatever seems to be outside of you, you then live in Heaven. Wherever God is, there is Heaven. And if God's Voice is all you hear, then you must be in Heaven.

When you hear God's Voice and use that Voice in your life, you are able to know Truth, easily make decisions, and move confidently in whatever direction you are guided. When you make a decision about how you want to live, when you commit to Peace over pain and Truth over illusion, it is very simple to know how to live in each moment and in every situation. Your own true religion is knowing yourself, knowing God and God's Will for you, believing and trusting in that, and allowing this Presence of Love within you to translate the language of the world into God's language, so that you may *be* that which you *are*, which is Love.

Hearing God's Voice is always available to everyone unconditionally. Choosing to hear this Voice is the key. Choosing is up to you. In Truth, you don't have a choice about God's Will. You don't have a choice about God's Voice or about that Voice being within you or part of you, but you can choose not to hear It. Beyond the choosing is the living. And it is dedication to choosing and living a certain way that allows you to experience the Truth of who you are.

Candace: DavidPaul and I are continually reminded by our Inner Voice *to live the Truth* that we are given. For us, hearing or knowing the Truth is not the hard part; it's applying the Truth to our lives and how we live that seems to be what we need help with the most.

It was on Christmas day, 1997, when we received our first communication about discovering and living our "true religion."

Greetings and blessings to you precious ones. Indeed this is a holy day and a most joyous occasion that we would gather together in this way on this most sacred of days. Every day can be this for you. Every day can be a holy day. Every day can be a sacred day. Today is one in which there is agreement on this. It is true that it is amazing that the world over is celebrating the anniversary of Jesus's birth today when perhaps on other days, most around the world would say that they don't even believe He ever existed, or exists now, or is in fact living in their hearts and minds. Yet there is some powerful momentum occurring within each one that builds and builds until this day comes when there is the understanding that "Peace on Earth, Goodwill toward Men" is indeed the ultimate. That each person would treat each other a little differently, that each one would be a little kinder, and that each one would be a little more generous, if only for one day or one time of year, is a miracle indeed.

The stories of scrooges being transformed into very generous people are stories that tend to occur only during this season. It is a season of transforming many of the aspects of yourself which you are not deeply in love with into aspects of yourself which you deeply love. It is a time of transforming all the areas of your life into exactly what you want them to be, so that what one is doing during this holy season is practicing a way to live—practicing kindness.

This is expressed by allowing someone to go ahead of them on the street or through a doorway. Donating money to good causes, donating time to be of service, being more honorable, charitable, or more in integrity in one's deeds, or letting go of seeming injustices and moving on are all examples of this. To show appreciation to those they love by purchasing things for them are acts of love to demonstrate their feelings ... to communicate with them, spend time with them, share words with family and friends that perhaps are not said throughout the year; and between lovers, to communicate those words that are often taken for granted or are presumed said when in fact the words are so lovely to hear.

This is a time of year to practice how one would want to be in all areas of their life. To plant the seeds of the perfection of the world during this time of year can carry you through and into the next year with the practice of kindness being at the foundation of your life.

When one attends a church service, it feels like a moment of honoring something that is perhaps important, and yet *living* a lifestyle and a practice of what is important to you *is* your religion. Many would say, "I am not religious. I am spiritual." Sometimes this is a way of not taking ownership or responsibility for a way of living. When one says their religion is Catholicism or Judaism, they are saying, "This is how I live." They are not saying, "This is a church service I have sat through, or a book I have read, or something my family spoke of," but a way of living.

When practicing Catholicism, certain prayers, masses, ritual, and ceremony are undertaken on a day-to-day basis, such as praying the rosary, taking Holy Communion, joining only in marriage, and so on. Doing certain things on certain days of the week is a way of honoring that which one sees as sacred, and a way of honoring that which one believes God has created. Regardless of whether or not you agree with these practices, performing them is a way of life; it is making a lifestyle around what one believes to be important.

Even if you do not agree with another's priorities, when one holds these priorities as high for themselves, they live a lifestyle that is in honor, integrity, and in grace with God through intention. There are many varieties of Christianity. Some include certain tenets around marriage, family, and other things based on individual priorities and values. Holy practices and beliefs are what bring about a sense of honor, tradition, connectedness for many.

To say that one is spiritual is to say that you are inherently an aspect of God. What does that look like as a lifestyle? What does that look like as a path? What practices does that involve so that you are living the lifestyle of "spirituality?" Do you see that when you say, "I am spiritual and not religious," this can be a way to avoid commitment to a certain lifestyle? One might say, "I am not religious because I am not Bible-oriented," and yet that is not the true definition of religious. These can be ways to escape the commitment to a lifestyle that you truly desire to make.

Perhaps today your goal would be to gently and lovingly notice what your priorities are. What is important to you? What matters to you? What feels like something you would not want to live without? Make a mental note of this and at the end of the day or as it occurs to you, you can make note of these priorities. Perhaps as you allow these to unfold you can discuss them and think about what would be your true religion. What would be a lifestyle and a way of practicing that which you love, that which is important to you and brings meaning to your life? How can you have ritual and ceremony and these sorts of things in such a way that you feel you have your true religion? It does not matter the name you call it. It does not matter what form it takes, only to think how you might like to live.

For the Dalai Lama, his true religion is kindness. You can see how every moment he would be able to ascertain, "What would be the best way to honor my religion in this moment?" And of course, that would be the kindest behavior in that moment. Now, sometimes, his religion can be difficult, because what may be the most kind in the moment may not look the most kind. Is it the most kind to you or is it the most kind to the other person? Is it the most kind to the planet, the most kind to God? Who is this kindness extended to?

The dilemma comes in when kindness must be originated toward self in order that it be extended outward as a result of the kindness extended inward. If your true religion is kindness, you must do what is most kind for yourself in each moment. Now it may be that what is being most kind for yourself is to deny yourself something or to experience something you might rather not for the sake of another. You can see how there is a continuous double-edged sword in the religion of kindness. Sometimes you must be kind to yourself and deny the other and sometimes kindness is denying yourself to give to the other. This is a constant challenge for one whose religion is kindness.

It might seem simple to discern what would be kind in every moment, and yet, it goes so much deeper—kind for whom, kind in what way, kind in that moment or kind over a lifetime, kind toward one's evolution or kind toward that present moment.

Let's say there are two people who have been in an accident and they have both stopped breathing. Which one do I give CPR to first? To whom would it be kind to give CPR? And which one would be the kindest? If these people have tuberculosis or some life threatening communicable disease, would it be kind for me to give them CPR and put my life in danger?

Having to determine in each moment what is kindness may not be as easy as one might think. What does kindness really mean? You may think it is kind to solve a problem for another person when in fact it could be the cruelest thing you do that day or week or lifetime because that person's mission or purpose for this whole lifetime was to figure out how to solve that problem on their own.

The Dalai Lama's true religion can be a source throughout his lifetime of discerning at every opportunity what is for the highest good of all. That is the way in which he serves himself in every situation. Develop your own religion and over time you will have this opportunity as well to determine, based on your priorities and your religion, what is truly for the highest good of all. You will be given this opportunity in every moment; it will be up to you to choose it.

Think about your priorities and make note of what they are. It is most important that you follow what is true for you, not what you think might be true for another, or what might please another, and certainly not what you think will please God. If you choose something, a priority, a goal, a lifestyle, or a religion to please God, in the end it will never work. You will have failed, and all your efforts will be for naught. Allow your priorities to unfold, and know that there is not a predetermined set or list that you must have. There are only those which are true in your heart.

Chapter Summary

The benefits of accessing our Inner Voice, by whatever name we call It, are endless. As we navigate through the challenges, judgment, and emotional pain we have in our daily lives, joining with this Presence within us has the ability to bring us true Peace, real Love, and genuine happiness. There is not a single painful experience we can bring to this Voice for Love that cannot instantly be healed or transformed as a result. It has the ability to guide us when we seek understanding and direction. It can help us develop a way of living in the world that is filled with integrity, fulfillment, and purpose. And It can restore our awareness to the Truth of Who We are and to our Oneness with All That Is—an ongoing state of awareness that one might call Enlightement.

The Barriers to Hearing Your Inner Voice

Though it is only a thought and not a step
that will bring you Home, God is
with you on the journey.

Because hearing God's Voice is your most natural state, it is easy to wonder what keeps you from It. In Truth, it is only a thought—a thought of separation, a thought of unworthiness, a thought that It is not real—and with that thought, God's Voice is gone from you.

Fortunately, it is only a thought. Fortunately, it only takes a thought to bring the Voice back to you—the thought that God's Voice is part of you, that God's Voice is your right, that God gave this Voice to you unconditionally. With those thoughts, you open the door to Truth.

Your mind just thinks. You can choose the thoughts you want to make real, and you can ignore the rest.

The Holy Spirit can help you discern which thoughts
you want to keep and which ones you want to ignore
until eventually you will only think thoughts of Truth.
You will only think with your Right-Mind.

WORTHINESS

DavidPaul: If hearing God's Voice is so natural, why did I
have to spend years struggling and going through hell trying
to hear You? Why are so many people confused about what
they hear or which voice they are hearing? What keeps us from
hearing this Voice as naturally as you say it is for us?

For so many, a barrier to God is a basic bottom line
thought or belief that one is not worthy of God and God's
Love. The thoughts can include that one is not good enough
for God to love, that one has been bad, one has sinned,
one has thought unlovingly about God, one has been angry
toward God, blamed God, judged God, and so on. All of these
thoughts would cause them to see themselves as unworthy of a
relationship with God. For many, they have been disappointed
by love. They feel that God has let them down or God has
disappointed them. God has hurt them and God has punished
them. There can be the idea that everything that goes "wrong"
in their life is God's fault, God's doing, God's meanness, or
God's wrath.

There is the idea that when one is sick or hurt they have
somehow done something wrong or disappointed God and
are being punished. The illness or injury is proof that they are
being punished by God, or proof that they are not loved or
worthy. The ego will seek proof everywhere. To the ego, an
illness, an injury, a divorce, or the death of a child or loved
one is all proof that God doesn't love them.

Everything that happens can be seen from whatever perspective you choose. There are some people who will look at things positively, others negatively, and some with the idea that what is happening is proof of either God's Love or God's punishment. If one believes that God doesn't love them or they're not worthy of God, then their whole life will become proof of that. Rather than living a happy life, they will prove their point. Many would rather be right than happy. That again is the power of the ego.

RELIGION

Another barrier to God might be the thought that one does not need God, or the thought that one does not want to be dependent on someone or something. Some people do not believe that God exists, while others do not understand the system of God, so they don't bother with it.

DavidPaul: What do you mean by system?

Either you pray and you love God, or you don't and you're punished. God will give you things if you pray in this way, and God won't if you don't. You must go to church at these times on these days and eat these things at these times and so on. It is so convoluted and so confusing for some that they would rather not bother because they don't understand the whole system. The system might mean religion or it might mean anything else.

For many, what would keep them from God is religion. Ironically, religion could be one of the greater barriers to God. There are many beliefs, or dogma, that cause people to feel unworthy and failing in their relationship with God. There are many expectations and perfect concepts of how to have a relationship with God and how to experience God. One must

E verything that happens can be
seen from whatever perspective
you choose.

speak in tongues on this particular day while they're spinning around three times and doing whatever else they are told. It is so difficult to reach the examples set for them or the rules established for them that many would run screaming from various religions in the world.

PERFECTION

Another common barrier is the misunderstanding about perfection. Many people don't understand that everything *is* perfect, and that when something happens, it is ultimately for the right reason. The original purpose of the world was to validate your separation from God, to make a place where God could not go so that you could have your autonomy. With Right-Mindedness, the world can serve another purpose as well. The world can be an opportunity to be reminded of who you are. With Right-Mindedness, the function of the world can serve a very high purpose indeed, and once you have been restored to the Truth of who you are, you will no longer need the world and it will fall away.

In the meantime, with Right-Mindedness, everything that happens in the world *is* perfection. With Right-Mindedness, you are able to perceive everything that is happening either through eyes of Love, so that you do not judge, or if you do judge, with ears of Love so that you can perceive the Truth of a situation rather than the illusion.

It is so easy for people to be confused and believe that when something bad happens, it is because they are bad, they are not loved, God doesn't love them, they've done something wrong, or they are being punished, rather than to try over time to see what good might possibly come of it.

Obviously, when one loses a child, you would not turn to them and say, "Try to see the positive." But over time, it may come to pass that those parents or siblings or grandparents or friends and family members might be able to appreciate the time that they had with that child and all that they received from that child, including all the joy, experiences, and laughter they would never have experienced otherwise. They may be grateful for what they did have and for the gift of that child in the world and have faith that for whatever reason that child's time in the world is complete. There may be other good things that come out of it, such as when a parent lobbies for laws to change or for conditions to shift around particular issues involving children based on what happened to their child.

It is easy to blame, be victimized, and suffer through what happens in the world and in life rather than to see the other side of it. With Right-Mindedness, whatever is happening in the world serves you in the goal of remembering the Truth of who you are. No matter what happens, it is exactly the right thing to serve you to that end. You can have faith and trust that whatever is happening is exactly as it should be to give you your goal of returning to God. You have made the world as the perfect reminder and the perfect pathway Home if you have the right perspective.

DavidPaul: Perfection is an easy concept to understand from a distance or when things are going as we would like, but when we wish things were different, it's another matter altogether. Over the years, we struggled with making this concept real in our lives, especially in our relationship. Consequently, we are sometimes reminded that Candace and I chose one another to overcome our most challenging issues, which is a nice way of saying that we often bring out the worst in one another.

When we first started to apply the concept of perfection in our relationship, we would often use it as justification or defense for not acknowledging each others' feelings and needs. For example, if Candace became annoyed with how dirty the house was and I didn't feel like dealing with her frustration and desire for a cleaner house, I might have flippantly said, "Must be perfect." This, of course, would lead to an eventful evening of passionate conversation.

While it is true that all things are perfect—the messy house, Candace's frustration, her desire for order, my judgment of her frustration and desire for order, my flippant comment, and the fight that ensued—this concept doesn't do us much good unless we know how to apply it to our lives, our thoughts, our emotions, and to every situation that comes to us. *Chapter 8 – Overcoming the Barriers to Hearing Your Inner Voice* will address how to apply this concept.

FEAR AND GUILT

If fear does indeed boil down to the possibility of losing what you have or not getting what you want, then people are frustrated by the idea that they cannot manipulate and control God for their own use. For example, someone will pray for something in the hope that they will get it. You *can* pray simply to talk with God, have connection and communion with God and your own sense of feeling good as a result of joining with God, or you can pray because you think you should, because you want or need something, or you've been told it is the thing to do. One will pray in the hope of getting on God's good side, and just that intention alone is a barrier. While one is praying in these ways, they are simultaneously building a barrier between themselves and God because of their intention and motivation for praying

When one lives in the world, rather than with God, the belief that they are their body and that the body can live or die causes one to feel vulnerable and dependant upon God for God's mercy and grace. Fear and resentment on this dependence can build. To think that your well-being is based on God's kindness is a scary thought. You then must do whatever it is you think you must do to stay in God's good grace so that your body may be spared from some illness or accident.

Some feel guilty that they seek God only in their time of need. When they are feeling desperate and on their knees, and they have the thought, "I only seek God in my hour of need. I haven't been thankful for anything. I haven't been grateful. I haven't connected with God for any other reason," they get up off their knees and walk away from that possible joining because of guilt. The thought is that they would have to pray more consistently in order to receive God's Goodness in their time of need. In that same situation, they might be on their knees not having joined with God in a very long time and feeling that it's been so long that God doesn't care about them or that God doesn't remember them because they haven't prayed enough and haven't been in union with God enough so they just aren't deserving of God. So even if they pray and even though God is right there holding them, rocking them, and loving them, they can't experience it because they don't believe they deserve it.

It's true that it doesn't matter what you think about God. If you don't believe in God, if you don't like God, if you don't understand God, if you don't care about God, that has nothing to do with God. And in fact, it has nothing to do with God's relationship with you. Just as someone can be in love with you and you don't have feelings for them, it is the same. God is in love with you and it doesn't matter how you feel about God; it doesn't change God's experience one bit. It is easy to think that you don't love God, therefore God doesn't love you. That couldn't be further from the Truth. You might think you don't know or understand God, therefore, how could God know or understand you. Again, that is not true.

✧

The original purpose of the world was to validate your separation from God, to make a place where God could not go so that you could have your autonomy. With Right-Mindedness, the world can serve another purpose as well. The world can be an opportunity to be reminded of who you are. With Right-Mindedness, the function of the world can serve a very high purpose indeed, and once you have been restored to the Truth of who you are, you will no longer need the world and it will fall away.

It is only your projections onto God that allow you to experience God in whatever ways you do. Those are based on your thoughts about yourself. When you don't like yourself very much, it is difficult to have a mutually rewarding, loving relationship with God. When you love and care about yourself, it is much easier to see that God loves and cares about you. When you judge or don't accept yourself, it is very difficult to imagine that God can accept you unconditionally.

Even when one understands what keeps them from the type of union with God that they truly seek in their heart, it doesn't mean that thoughts won't pop up that try to keep you from joining with God. When you notice what you're thinking, such as, "Hmmm, I haven't been connecting with God frequently enough," you can ask yourself, "Is that true? Does God care? I'm here with God now and there is no time and space. This is the only moment there is and here I am with God. Thank you, God, for always being here for me to join with. Thank you for receiving me in this and all moments." You can then experience your connection with God no matter what thoughts arise.

When you are able to notice that you are having a thought that is distracting you away from God, recognize that it is just a thought. It's not true now, nor has it ever been. The only Truth is that you are One with God, that God loves you just as you are and is completely aware of your Perfection that has never changed. Any thought you have that takes you away from God couldn't be true; it's just not possible. Acknowledge it for what it is. Let it go, and rejoin with God. Sit back down on God's Lap, settle in, get comfy, and feel God's Arms around you. Just lean back and enjoy it.

There is the idea that only people who have studied religion for many years could ever be worthy of actually hearing God. Many people have the belief that only the Pope might receive some direct communication from God, only one who is more deserving or more sin free can hear. Neale Donald Walsch (author of the *Conversations with God* series) is one person who openly admits to hearing God and shares his conversations with God in books. He might be considered an example of the idea that if he can do it, anybody can. In Truth, everyone can and does.

Some have experienced fear when hearing things and haven't trusted what they heard. Some have heard things that were frightening or that didn't make sense, so they stopped hearing. Some may have heard a grandparent who has passed on whisper something in their ear and it frightened them. It may have been a very sweet and loving communication, but it was frightening nonetheless. One may have heard God communicating to them as a child or in some other situation, and again it was just a frightening experience because it was unfamiliar, so one stops their ability to hear. It is as if they turn that off somehow.

There are many who are fearful of what they might hear. They have heard that someone went out and murdered 68 people because God told them to. There are some who are afraid that if they hear God's Voice, they may be told something like that. For some, they may have tried and didn't hear and then became invalidated and gave up. There are some who have tried and tried and tried and tried and tried and tried and tried and tried, and they may even be hearing God, and they just don't realize it because they're trying so hard to hear It a certain way. They are so frustrated with the whole experience that their frustration distracts them away from God's Voice.

There are some who believe that to hear God you must follow a certain set of rules, or there might be only one established pathway for hearing God and they're not on it. There may be an incident in their past that they can't let go of, and when they sit down to talk to God, that issue is at the forefront of their mind and they are not able to hear. For some,

When you are able to notice that you are having a thought that is distracting you away from God, recognize that it is just a thought. It's not true now, nor has it ever been.... Acknowledge it for what it is. Let it go, and rejoin with God.

there is just enough chatter, unfinished conversations, and thoughts floating around in one's head that there is actually too much noise to hear God talking. For many people, sitting alone, being still, focusing on breathing, quieting the mind, and letting go of all of the things that have to be done is very difficult.

Again, there are more than seven billion barriers to hearing God. These are just a few.

JUDGMENT

DavidPaul: Judgment is another common barrier to hearing God's Voice. As soon as we judge, no matter how big or small the judgment may be, we simultaneously experience the pain of feeling separate. For most of us, these judgments are so habitual and pervasive that we become numb to the pain we cause ourselves by judging—at least this has been the case for me.

While Candace and I were still living in Hawaii, my humbling experience of trying to will myself into enlightenment once and for all brought me to the realization that I had no idea how to get myself out of the hole I had so willfully dug. I didn't understand why I felt so lifeless, nor did I know how to breathe any life back into me.

It was during this time of feeling so incredibly stuck that Candace started hearing this Voice within her on the Big Island. Feeling as if I had nowhere else to turn, I visited her to see if somehow the Holy Spirit could bring me back to life. We spent the entire weekend in a flurry of activity, swimming with dolphins, touring the island, visiting the volcano. Before we knew it, Candace was driving me back to the airport. She had wanted to give me communication from God's Voice, but there had been no time to do it.

We arrived at the airport thirty minutes early and sat down

on a small patch of grass to wait for my plane's boarding call. As we did, Candace closed her eyes and began to speak—it was the first time I had ever heard Candace share God's Voice before. Sitting there on the grass, the Holy Spirit began to talk with me about "desire" and the opportunity to embrace it with love and acceptance rather than judgment. Since landing on Kauai, I had slowly and methodically judged and eradicated every thought that arose within me, including my desires— my desire to play, explore, learn, meet people, interact, and be in the world. I destroyed them all, banished them from my mind to try to maintain my awareness of Truth, or at least I thought I banished them. In reality, I buried them under layers of judgment not knowing how else to integrate my experience of Truth into the world.

As God spoke to me about my desires, I was lead out of the misery I made with my judgmental thinking and into an experience of embracing the desires within me in such a way that I no longer saw them as something to push away or avoid, but as beautiful thoughts to embrace. In one magical moment of listening to God's Voice, the incessant and unconscious judgments that I had been harboring toward my desires suddenly fell away. What was left was an all-consuming passion within me to fully embrace those thoughts as a friend, to fully accept and allow my desires to exist without judgment. It was the first of many life changing experiences hearing this Voice.... I missed my plane, but it was worth it.

THOUGHT

DavidPaul: Everything You have said so far about the barriers to hearing God's Voice within us seems like a thought or belief of some kind. Can you talk about the power of thought and how our thoughts impact our reality?

Thought is the most powerful form of creation in the world. What one thinks, they may come to believe. What one believes, they may come to make real in the world. And it is the thought that one attaches to which becomes real, that then shapes the world and the way one sees it.

Everything is a thought. Your concept of yourself is a thought. Your concept of your partner is a thought, which may be a whole large number of thoughts all put together to form this person who you perceive as your partner. Your home, your family, your job, the world, and everyone and everything in it are thoughts; and on top of those, you then have thoughts you think about everyone and everything in the world.

Thoughts come and thoughts go. They mostly keep moving. Then one will arise, and it will be as if you have latched onto that thought, and then that thought becomes real. Rather than just a concept floating by, it now begins to take on meaning. With the meaning that you give that thought, it then begins to become a belief, which means with the way you experience that thought and the power you give it, you now have certain rules and experiences attached to that thought, which forms the world as you know it.

Let's say, for example, that you have the belief that you *are* a body. Another might have the belief that they are a spirit who *has* a body. Then, on top of that belief, there is the belief that the body gets hungry. Then on top of that, there is the belief that the body needs food and water to survive. Then there is the belief that certain foods are good and certain foods are not; certain foods cause you to feel this way and certain foods do not; some may generate health, while others in your belief system may cause you to become ill; certain foods may be fattening and some may be energizing; and so on.

All of these are thoughts that you have attached to that you now believe are true about you. And even though there are studies that prove that a certain food is good for you or bad for you, that study is a thought as well, or a belief if you attach to it. Whether or not you know what really happened in that study or the people and circumstances surrounding it, whether you heard a statistic or a quoted fact, now you believe that almonds are good for you and you eat almonds. You may or may not perceive a benefit in the body, and then you hear of another study that says that almonds are fattening or that many people are allergic to them or that in some way they are not beneficial, so you stop eating them. You do not know if anything you have been told about almonds is true. You just believe it, and then apply that belief to your body, which is just a thought as well. This is one tiny example of one's whole experience of living in the world.

This is true of your experience of God as well. All of the thoughts that one has about God are what makes their reality of God. If you believe God is loving, then your God is loving. If you believe that God is angry and vengeful, then your God is angry and vengeful. The mind thinks thoughts and the ego attaches to those thoughts, gives them meaning, invents belief systems, and then manifests a world based on those thoughts and belief systems. The Holy Spirit, on the other hand, corrects the perception of the thought so that you see the Truth, which is ultimately that the thought itself is not true, and therefore everything associated with that thought is not true either.

In Reality, you are not the body and the body does not exist. You might think, "Hmm, I am not the body. I am a spirit living in a body." Then you may go one step further and think, "Hmm, bodies are something I dreamed up to walk me through the world I dreamed up."

The Holy Spirit's job is to show you that, in fact, the body isn't real and every belief associated with the body, therefore, cannot be real. So as you begin to undo this house of cards, which are the beliefs you have surrounding the body, and as it all comes crashing down, you can begin to have the

Thought is the most powerful form of creation in the world. What one thinks, they may come to believe. What one believes, they may come to make real in the world. And it is the thought that one attaches to which becomes real, that then shapes the world and the way one sees it.

experience that, in fact, you don't have a body—or at least you cannot know if you have a body. You cannot know then if it needs to eat. You cannot know what is good for it and what isn't. At that point, all you can do is follow your heart. And when you have the thought to get up and prepare some food for your body, you just get up and prepare the food and eat it, and there are no thoughts associated with what is right or wrong for you. And it is one step closer to stepping out of the world and waking up from the dream.

Candace: When I first started hearing God's Voice within me in Hawaii, I had little understanding of the impact that our thinking can have on hearing this Voice. At the time, my experience of hearing this Voice was simple and natural. It was just there—a constant companion that I could join with and listen to anytime I wanted.

As time went on, I continued doing sessions with others since I committed in the beginning to always say yes. Because the messages were equally applicable to me and because I could already hear this Voice, I came to believe that sharing this Voice with others was all I needed to do to keep my own life on track. As a result, I soon stopped listening to this Voice within me on my own.

I would tune into the Holy Spirit for a session with someone else and then "turn It off" when I was done. Soon, I was no longer listening to this Loving Presence throughout the day. I became more enmeshed in the world and lost my foothold in Reality. I forgot who I was, why I was here, and that God's Child was all around me. I was listening to the ego more and more and believing what I saw with my eyes. As a result of believing that sharing God's Voice was all I needed to do to keep my life on track, I stopped having my own relationship with this Voice and soon lost my sense of connection with It.

✧ EXERCISE – THOUGHT VS. REALITY

It is helpful to become aware of your thoughts so that you can understand how you are affected by what you think, even though most of what you think may not be true. For example, when you wake up in the morning, you may have a thought about how much sleep you did or did not get and how that is going to impact your day. You may look out the window and have a thought about the weather and what that is going to mean. You might begin thinking about everything that you need to do that day. As a result, you are already in the future, rather than in this moment of waking up and welcoming a new day, connecting with yourself, Truth, or God's Voice within you, and just being thankful for a new day.

You might begin thinking about what you are going to have for breakfast, whether or not you need a shower, what you are going to wear, and all of the things that you need to get done once you get up—the phone calls that must be made, a card that needs to be sent, or something to be purchased along with all the work that has to get done. Before you know it, you are overwhelmed, exhausted, and sad or frustrated with all that you have to do, when the reality is, you are just lying in bed, yawning, stretching, and coming alive.

Once you become aware of your thoughts, you can then notice the opportunity to give thanks for a new day, connect with yourself and God, and appreciate what *is* in that moment. As the thoughts of the day begin to creep in, you can remind yourself of what you are actually doing—breathing, stretching, perhaps getting out of bed, maybe standing up and putting one foot in front of the other—without overwhelming yourself with your thinking. Notice how often this occurs during the day and remind yourself that it is *just a thought*. Remind yourself of what your reality truly *is* in that moment. You are lying in bed, waking up, or simply picking up peaches at the store. You have no worries, no fears, no suffering, and you can enjoy each moment you are able to remember that.

CHAPTER SUMMARY

There are countless barriers to hearing God's Voice, but no matter what we come up with, they all have one thing in common. They are all just thoughts—thoughts of fear, judgment, or unworthiness; a belief, concept, or perception. It doesn't matter what form the barriers take. They are all just a thought in one form or another.

Fortunately, it is only a thought that keeps us from hearing God's Voice, and we can choose which thoughts we want to listen to.

– 8 –

Overcoming the Barriers to Hearing Your Inner Voice

There is no difference between love and healing.
They are one and the same. They are each
accomplished by the other in the mind.

There are a wide variety of thoughts that keep one from hearing God's Voice, and yet, they are all just thoughts. Because thoughts are so powerful, they each seem to take on a power of their own and seem to mean something different that must be overcome or understood or solved. But a thought is just a thought, regardless of the meaning you give it, and every thought that keeps you from hearing Truth has an opposite thought that can open the door to Truth. Therefore, it is very simple to overcome the barriers to hearing God because those barriers are just a thought and you can always choose to think differently. The challenge is in noticing that you are having a thought that does not serve you. It has become so comfortable and familiar to think thoughts that take you away from the Truth that noticing them is now the difficulty.

With awareness, intention, practice, and determination, you can become aware of what you are thinking and make a decision about what you want to think. The more you do it, the easier it becomes … until one day it is just a way of life.

SELF-AWARENESS

DavidPaul: I struggled for so many years trying to hear this Voice within me. Looking back on it now, I can clearly see the tiny misperceptions, expectations, and beliefs that I unconsciously held which kept me from hearing God's Voice in the way that I do today. God, how do we begin to uncover these thoughts within us? What can one do to overcome these barriers more quickly and easily than I did?

To overcome the barriers to hearing God, you must first recognize that what you are hearing is not God and you must have the desire to hear God. At some point, the noise of the world becomes so shrill, loud, and invasive that one becomes aware that they are not enjoying what they are hearing and thinks that perhaps there might be a better way.

It is easy to forget about God and be distracted by the pace and temptations of the world. There is a very deep part of you that is nagging you to remember that this is just a dream. A sincere desire to connect with God and God's Voice will ultimately take you there. In Truth, that is all you could desire because that is the Truth of who you are and the Truth of your heritage. Since you have never been separate, that is all you seek to remember.

Take notice of your life, your body, your health, and anything within your body that is not effortless and pain-free. Take notice of your home, your family, your work, your finances, and your part in society. Then take note of you and how you feel on a day-to-day basis. You may have everything that the world says you should have to be happy, and yet you may not be happy. Or you may have everything and think you are happy, yet you find yourself angry much of the time. You may have few of the things the world says you need in order to be happy and you may be resentful or sad about that. Your health may be seriously compromised, or you may hold thoughts all day of attack, blame, and judgment.

How you think and feel are the keys to how you are really doing. If your mind is happy, if you are at peace, if you are contented with your life, accepting of your neighbor, understanding of yourself and your family, and loving what is, then you know that you have a strong foothold in Reality, which is not of this world. If you are unhappy, depressed, sad, angry, resentful, or guilty, or if you are judging your neighbors, disconnected from your family, mad at the world, or wishing that things were different, then you can be assured that your mind is not with God. You are not in your Right-Mind.

If you are on a continual quest for more—more money, more stuff, more time, more love, more joy—that is a sign to you that your thinking is not working for you and that, in Truth, what you seek is more connection with God. You can go out in pursuit of more of this and that for the rest of your life and what you are ultimately seeking is more connection with God. Once you become aware of that, you stop, you sit, you say hello to God, and you connect with God in that instant.

You know there are barriers between you and God any time you are not happy, fulfilled, contented, at peace, or accepting and understanding of what is. If there is not peace in your life, then it is time to stop and connect.

Once you become aware that it is only your thinking that is a barrier to God, it can be very easy to restore your mind to Truth, because awareness is a huge piece of the puzzle. Once you become aware that your thinking is not working for you, then you can begin the search for Right-Thinking.

SELF-INQUIRY

As you become more aware of your thoughts, you also become more aware of your beliefs. As you begin to question these beliefs, knowing that nothing in the world is True or Real, you can begin to shed the beliefs that have weighed you down for so long and kept you from your communication with God. When you question the beliefs that you hadn't realized caused you pain, you come to understand that maybe what you always thought was true, isn't in fact true, and one link is removed from the chain that has held you down.

As you become aware of more and more beliefs, something as simple as boys think this way or girls feel that way to something as complicated as death is final, and you question these beliefs, you release the chains that have bound you and become more free of the world each time. The more free of the world you become, the more opportunity for God to take the place of those beliefs—God being Love or Truth or Reality.

As an example, in asking, "Is it true that winter is cold, lonely, and depressing?" you may come to find that winter may be the same as any other season, that there are many gifts and miracles in winter, or that wintertime is an opportunity to go within, hibernating as a bear might, and letting go or changing a belief so that it now serves you and gives you a tremendous sense of freedom. Eventually, the more you

To overcome the barriers to hearing God, you must first recognize that what you are hearing is not God and you must have the desire to hear God.

question your thoughts about winter, the more you will come to understand that winter is just a thought. From a place of Truth or Reality, every day will be the same for you, and whatever is in front of you will be perfect. You will not judge or evaluate what is in front of you. It will just be. Eventually, you will get to the point of not labeling what is in front of you at all and simply allow yourself to be present and experience love, true understanding, true acceptance, and the peace and joy that come with that.

It is a freedom from the world that the deepest part of you seeks, knowing that in overcoming the world, all that is left is God, which is all there ever has been and all there ever will be. You have just forgotten. As you overcome the world and your Oneness is remembered and restored, the ego is forgotten. It is as if it never existed, because in Truth, it never did, right along with the world, and you are left to revel in your Wholeness, your Completeness, your Oneness with all that is, without question, just Joy.

Candace: Because the Holy Spirit works with our mind as well as God's, It will speak directly to us and through us to other people using what is already in our mind—phrases, experiences, thoughts, and expressions that are uniquely ours. I first began to notice this after spending a number of years doing "The Work of Byron Katie," which is a process of writing down our judgments, questioning them, and then "turning them around" so they can be seen from a different perspective. After several years of practicing The Work, I noticed different aspects of The Work coming through me when I listened to God's Voice or shared this Voice with others.

The Work, which I discovered the same month I began hearing God's Voice in April 1994, has been a very powerful process in my life. It is based upon self-inquiry, and I have used it to undo my beliefs about my family, my body, my relationships, and my life, and have gained tremendous freedom in all of these areas from understanding the Truth of my thinking. Like listening to God's Voice within you, the Work is a process that has the ability to take one directly to Right-Mindedness.

✧ EXERCISE – CAN YOU REALLY KNOW?

If you have doubts or fears about your ability to hear God's Voice, make a list of those doubts and fears. It might include:

1. God isn't real.
2. I will never hear God's Voice.
3. This Voice for Love is not inside of me.
4. I am not worthy of hearing God's Voice.
5. God doesn't love me so I don't have this Voice within me.
6. And so on....

Then, with each one of these beliefs, begin to question whether or not you can really know if that is true. Can you really know that God is not real? Can you really know that you won't be able to hear God's Voice? Can you know definitively that you are not worthy of God, God's Voice, or God's Love?

As you ask yourself these questions, you may come to realize that you cannot know if these thoughts are true or not. Begin to open your mind to the possibility that, in fact, you might be mistaken. Begin to open your mind to the possibility that God *does* exist, you *will* hear God's Voice, you *do* hear God's Voice, you *are* worthy of God and God's Love, and that this Voice for Love *is* within you. Focus on these possibilities rather than the others.

It's just as likely that these answers are true and, in fact, much more likely. You may as well put your faith into that which is hopeful and enjoyable to believe, knowing ultimately

As you overcome the world and your Oneness is remembered and restored, the ego is forgotten. It is as if it never existed, because in Truth, it never did, right along with the world, and you are left to revel in your Wholeness, your Completeness, your Oneness with all that is, without question, just Joy.

that it has to be true because, in Reality, only God, God's Child, and God's Voice exist.

USE WHAT WORKS

Self-awareness and self-inquiry are simple practices, but they are not necessarily easy. The ego is amazingly good at its job. As a result, countless practices have been created with the intention to heal our minds, experience Truth, understand ourselves, undo our beliefs, overcome the ego, and be in the present moment. These practices range from a wide variety of meditation and self awareness methods to physical disciplines such as yoga, tai chi, and many others. Support groups, spiritual and religious organizations, prayer, professional counseling, talking with friends and family, reading spiritual or self-help books, and following our hearts and dreams are but a few of the things we can do that also have the potential to help bring awareness to our minds.

The list of methods and techniques for overcoming the ego is far-reaching. Ultimately, all methods that restore us to Right-Mindedness are a blessing, and this Voice for Truth within us will work with anything to accomplish this. Because restoring our minds to Right-Thinking *is* the function of the Holy Spirit, we can also join directly with this Inner Voice as a way of undoing the thoughts and beliefs that keep us from having the relationship with our Self and God that we truly long for.

USING YOUR INNER VOICE

DavidPaul: I was lucky to have Candace in my life sharing God's Voice with me all those years to finally uncover and begin hearing this Inner Voice for myself. How can other people use *their* Inner Voice to accomplish the same goal?

Since God has given everyone His Voice inside of them, it is then equally possible for all of God's children to connect with Truth and Right-Mindedness through the Holy Spirit. God gave His Children an Interpreter, one who could see all sides of things, understand the temptations of the ego versus the Truth in ways that God does not comprehend or cannot talk to you about because God does not perceive the ego. There are no restorations to make from God's perspective. There is just connection and Oneness.

Restoring yourself to Right-Mindedness can happen instantly as you connect with God through your own doing, or it can happen through the work of the Holy Spirit by asking this Voice within you to help restore your mind to Right-Thinking. You can ask this Inner Teacher to be with you and to share with you a perspective of Truth to guide, direct, and comfort you in the ways of Reality rather than illusion. You can ask this Comforter to hold your hand and give you that which you need to maneuver your way around the world as you make your way to God.

You can use Jesus in the same way by asking Him to be with you, to help you restore your mind to Right-Thinking, to hold your hand as you walk through the world, afraid but growing in Faith, with the desire for your Oneness to be restored to you. What Jesus did in his lifetime as Jesus was to think only with the thinking of his Right-Mind, rather than with the thinking of the ego. By doing that, Jesus overcame the world and is in your heart and mind to mentor you in the same way. Jesus is an example of what it looks like in an earthly form to think only with the Right-Mind, so that you can know it is possible to hear only God through the Holy Spirit. If you are hearing God's Voice, you cannot hear the ego. If you hear the ego, you cannot hear God's Voice at the same time—they do not talk over each other.

The ego does not get destroyed in the process of hearing God's Voice; it just becomes dormant. You can hear God's Voice at all times if that is what you seek. You can have that be the only Voice you hear. That does not mean you have annihilated the ego in the process. It means you choose, in every moment, the Holy Spirit, the Voice for Truth, the Comforter, the Call to Joy, and the ego soon becomes a quiet and powerless voice in the back of your mind.

BEFRIENDING YOUR THOUGHTS

Thoughts themselves are not the enemies. It is only what you do with a thought that can harm you. You can ignore a thought, question a thought, believe a thought, act on a thought … all of these are up to you. Thoughts come and thoughts go. That is the mind's job. What you do with the thoughts is your choice.

Thoughts are innocent in and of themselves and have no power, no meaning, and no impact. It is what you do with a thought that gives it meaning. If you have a thought that you like, you can hold onto that thought. You can believe it. You can act on it and enjoy what you get from it. If you have a thought that you do not like, you need not be a victim to it, but rather you can question it. Is that thought true? Can you really know that whatever it is you are thinking is true? And if it does not serve you to keep that thought, then let it go.

As one begins to work on their mind, they may perceive all of their thoughts as enemies. The truth is … thought creates. You were created from a Thought of God, and everything in your world was made from a thought. Rather than presuming that every thought you have is an enemy or will distract you from Truth or keep you from that which you truly seek, you can instead meet every thought as an innocent friend.

If you have a thought that you do not like for whatever

reason, you can thank the thought for existing and allow it to go on its way. It is not bad just because *you* don't like it. Another person may have the same thought and enjoy it, keep it, believe it, and act on it. Thoughts are not inherently good or bad. That is determined by the meaning you give them. Presuming they are all innocent, you meet them and greet them, and you keep the ones you like and you let go of the ones you do not, not from a place of anger, purging, or fear, but from a place of cleaning out, just as you would clean out your cupboards in the spring. It is not because something is good or bad that you would get rid of it. It is because it no longer serves a purpose for you and you let it go. You make room for new things that you like more.

This is easily accomplished from a place of Right-Mindedness, but even without that, you can still sit patiently and lovingly, and as each thought comes to you, greet it, welcome it, examine it, and then kindly keep it or let it go. There is no fear in this. There is no urgency, anger, or hatred. There is only acceptance, understanding, love, and peace, and that is what you would seek in any situation. Apply it to your thoughts, and you will watch it manifest in your life in amazing and wonderful ways.

EMBRACING ALL THINGS

The Holy Spirit once told us that the Temple of the Holy Spirit is not a body but a relationship. At the time, we thought the Holy Spirit was only referring to relationships between people because we first heard this communication when we initially became a couple. After years of hearing this Voice within us and learning how to apply It's Wisdom to our lives, we now understand that the Holy Spirit was referring to our relationship with *all things*, not just with each other. This includes every

If you are hearing God's Voice, you cannot hear the ego. If you hear the ego, you cannot hear God's Voice at the same time—they do not talk over each other.

thought, emotion, feeling, and belief that we perceive to be within us *and* every situation, idea, and physical object we perceive to be outside of us.

This concept is especially powerful when we practice creating a Holy Relationship with our inner thoughts. If we can stop judging, suppressing, and trying to control our thoughts, and instead create a Holy Relationship with them, we can completely rewire the way we relate to ourselves and the world.

When a thought comes up, welcome it. Befriend it. Bless it. Extend love or kindness to it. When we do, we are *being* the Holy Spirit in the world. We are perceiving our thoughts for what they truly are... just thoughts. Innocent. Meaningless. Powerless. It is only through our judgment that we give our thoughts all the impact, meaning, and power that they have for us. When we create a Holy Relationship with our thoughts, there is nothing to solve, nothing to fix, nothing to heal ... and only Love remains.

DavidPaul: After the life changing communication I received from God about embracing my desires at the Kona airport that day with Candace, I stepped off the plane on Kauai full of passion and life once again. I went from an apathetic, lifeless man to one on a mission to befriend and embrace his desires. While I won't go into unnecessary details, having nearly withered away to a mere 110 pounds upon my arrival at Candace's doorstep, food and my joyful and gluttonous embracing of it soon become a wonderful pastime.

Since my new goal in life was to fully embrace my desires without judgment as completely as possible, I went to the grocery store one night after work and bought 16 double packages of Reese's peanut butter cups. I went home, meditated a bit, and then proceeded to slowly and consciously savor each delicious cup as if it was the only thing that existed in the world. It took me two hours to consume all 32 cups, not because I was full or because they were making me sick, but because I was completely joining with every ounce of flavor and experience I could allow myself to feel. It was amazing.

The following week, I performed the same ritual with Ben & Jerry's Chocolate Fudge Brownie ice cream, this time slowly devouring 3 pints in one glorious sitting. By fully embracing my desires with unconditional love and acceptance, I came to notice that my desires rarely returned. To this day, I have no desire for candy bars or ice cream, not because I had eaten too much of them, but because I fully embrased those desires within me with unconditional love and acceptance. I haven't purchased a candy bar or a pint of ice cream ever since. The desire to do so just doesn't exist.

After several months of enjoying my gluttony and living out every desire I truly wanted, my passion and joy began to plateau, and I started getting restless. I immediately recognized the warning signs and called Candace to ask for communication from the Holy Spirit. Much to my surprise, the communication I received was similar to what I received before, but instead of talking about desire, the Holy Spirit spoke to me about feeling my emotions. It was the same principle—learning how to love and embrace my emotions without judgment—just as I had done with my desires.

For much of my life, I viewed emotion as something to either overcome or express. As soon as I became aware of an emotion, I would immediately judge its value. Do I get rid of it, or do I take a stand? If the answer was getting rid of it, I typically stuffed it or willed myself out of having it. If the emotion seemed honorable, justifiable, or worth fighting for, I'd throw on my armor and go to battle, either subtly or not so subtly. Either way I chose, peace and freedom still eluded me.

As I listened to God's Words over the phone with Candace, the unconscious judgments I had been harboring toward my emotions were immediately released. What was left was a bounding sense of joy and passion. During the call, I was led

It is not because something is good or bad that you would get rid of it. It is because it no longer serves a purpose for you and you let it go. You make room for new things that you like more.

through an exercise of feeling my emotions. I then practiced this exercise each day for several months.

First, I would close my eyes and find a safe and secure connection to Truth within me. Anchored in this connection, I would then imagine a water faucet in front of me. As I turned the valve, my emotions would begin to flow through me. Maintaining my connection with Truth and Right-Mindedness, I would then allow myself to embrace the emotions that came. Very similar to the exercise of eating peanut butter cups and ice cream, I would feel, with all of my attention, every emotion that arose—fear, anger, hatred, sadness—often sobbing for long periods of time throughout the exercise.

Being anchored in Right-Mindedness while simultaneously feeling my emotions allowed me to witness the rising and falling away of my emotions without judgment. While I assumed they were connected to or the result of some triggering thought or perception, instead of focusing on the cause of the emotion, I just felt them. If I noticed myself identifying, judging, trying to understand, evaluate, or do anything but feel the emotions that arose within me, I would immediately return my attention to *only* feeling. That was my only goal and focus.

At first, it was frightening to feel my emotions so strongly. Tears would often stream down my face for twenty or thirty minutes straight. Then, the tears would stop and into me would flow a deep sense of peace and joy. It was an intense practice, and yet the cycle was always the same: intense emotion followed by incredible peace. When I was ready, I would open my eyes, get up, and go about my day feeling refreshed, alive, and on top of the world.

After several months, the idea of lovingly embracing my desires and emotions without judgment began to spread and I started to see the possibility of embracing every thought with the same intention and perspective. As this possibility took root, I began to lose the distinction between my inner thoughts, emotions, and beliefs and those seemingly outside of me, like my body, another person, or a physical thing or event in the world. From my new perspective, they were all equal. They were all a thought in one form or another, and I could apply this practice to all of them equally.

Eventually, as my desire to embrace and experience all things without judgment began to blossom within me, I knew in my heart that my time in Hawaii had come to an end. I had given myself the gift of coming to understand how it was possible to live in Truth while simultaneously living in the illusion of the world. It was now time to apply this concept to every area of my life, every thought in my mind, and every moment of my day.

Little did I know how difficult that would be.

REMEMBERING HOW TO PLAY

Candace: Playing and having fun with my daughter seems to impact my ability to stay connected with my Inner Voice. When I feel stressed out or overwhelmed, I feel much more disconnected. Can you talk about the role that playing has in hearing God's Voice in our lives?

Play is just an acknowledgment to lighten up and not take things so seriously. One can have their Oneness with God and still be incredibly serious and heavy. Even with a certain sense of freedom from the world, there is still a life or death type of experience people can bring to their relationship with God or to their spirituality.

Play is an invitation to simply lighten up, to play as little children with God, and to play in the world. You came here truly to play. Yes, it is a school, but school is not about work. It is about growing, learning, exploring, investigating, making friends, and doing different things. And if that's the case, then lighten up and play and have some fun.

There are kids who spend their day studying, learning, trying, being in effort, and doing homework and extra projects. They could have some fun and not take it so seriously. You learn what you need to learn, and you won't learn what you don't need to learn. Most of it is not True or Real anyway. Just try to have some fun and know that you will always learn what you need to learn.

There is the idea for many that they need to prove to God their commitment, their dedication, or their loyalty, and this is done through seriousness. The one who serves Jesus is the one who sits at his feet and listens to him and connects with him, rather than the one who "serves" him food or drink. The one who serves him food or drink is also present with him. It is a tremendous service to "play" with another in this way. It is a beautiful way of being present with another, being in the moment and having this thought and going with it or having that thought and going with it.

When one is playing, there are no problems. There are no fears. There are no worries. There is very little in the way of illusion and very much in the way of happiness, fulfillment, peace, and love.

CHAPTER SUMMARY

There are two thought systems. The ego's thought system and the Holy Spirit's thought system. One causes pain. The other brings Peace. One is a barrier to hearing God's Voice. The Other *is* God's Voice.

To overcome the barriers to hearing God's Voice, one must first become aware that what they are thinking or feeling in any given moment is painful. Self-Awareness—being aware of our present moment experience—is therefore an important first step to hearing God's Voice within us. For most of us, we are used to the ego's thought system. We believe it. We rationalize it. We are addicted to it, and we prove its validity over and over again each time we choose it. When we step back within our mind and notice that what we are thinking or feeling in any given moment is painful, we become empowered to relate to the ego differently. We become empowered to question the ego's validity or reality. And we become willing to receive all that God's Voice has to give us.

– 9 –

Opening the Door

Prayer opens the door and God is waiting patiently on the other side of that door, at all times, in all situations, to join with you.

It is easy to misunderstand prayer, how to use it, and its purpose and function while living in the world. Regardless of what one prays for, prayer has only one true function. Regardless of what one seeks, prayer can only be used in one way. It does not matter to whom you pray, how you pray, or why you pray, God is the only Source, and your prayer opens the door to Him.

STARTING THE DIALOGUE

Candace: Talking to God has always been part of my life, although I never thought of it as "prayer." Can you explain the purpose of prayer and how we can use it to hear this Voice more clearly in our lives?

Prayer is one of the greatest tools one can have in the world because it opens the door to a dialogue with God. To pray is to know to whom you are speaking, rather than the form it takes. Prayer means that one is engaged in a dialogue with God in particular, and/or God's Voice. Prayer means that you are beginning a dialogue with the One Who created you, the One who never left you, and you are reestablishing that connection within your mind, within your heart, and giving yourself the opportunity to have a deeper experience with Source. Prayer is the opportunity to transcend the world in any given moment and connect with what is really True and Real. When one chooses prayer, one is choosing to step aside from all that seems to be happening and seek connection with their Father.

If you say a prayer to God and you stop for a moment and connect with God, acknowledge God, thank God, or appreciate God in the course of that prayer, its function will have been fulfilled. If you say a prayer without acknowledging God or connecting with God in some way, then the function of the prayer is not fulfilled. It does not matter what is prayed for and it does not matter what the outcome of the specific request is because the function of the prayer is to connect with God, to remember Truth, to overcome the dream in that moment. This is not necessarily acknowledged or understood in the moment, but by asking something of One Whom you've never seen and have no proof of, just by that act, you are overcoming the world.

If you say a prayer because you think you should, because it is the right thing to do, because it couldn't hurt, or out of an obligation or responsibility, again the prayer does not fulfill its function. A prayer can be as simple as "Hello, God" or "Thank You, God" or it can be an unending dialogue about anything you want to share with God. Prayer need not happen in a physical church, but in the church within you. If you are walking down the street, driving in your car, or shopping in a store, and you have the thought to say hello to God, thank

God, or ask for something in as light-hearted and casual a way or as serious a way as you feel called, it is all the same.

Many believe they must be serious and reverent in their prayers with God, and yet that is unnecessary. Remembering God in a happy moment as well as a challenging moment is a wonderful blessing for everyone, and to connect with God in whatever place you are is always welcome.

Prayer is necessary in the process of hearing God's Voice. It is not that you must get on your knees and pray the rosary this many times a day in these particular ways and then you will someday hear God. Prayer is what opens the dialogue. One person has to start talking for another person to talk back. It does not matter who talks first, what is said, where, how, or anything else, though as long as two people sit silently, no dialogue will occur. It could be said that God talks to you at all times, and at some point, you acknowledge that and you talk back and that is prayer. Then you hear God more specifically because you are now engaged in the conversation. Once you start a conversation through prayer, whatever that looks like, the relationship begins.

Obviously one can pray to many things, but prayer is always directed toward Source or Creator. So whether one calls that the Sun, the Earth, Allah, Buddha, Christ, God, or Jesus, it does not matter. Prayer is being directed to the same Source, to the Creator of what is Real, and it is a way of asking to transcend the world.

When one prays, they are opening the door to communication with God and seeking a connection with what is Real. They are trying to get past their experience of the world, of the dream, and to remind themselves of what is True. Prayer is the opportunity to talk with God, and God hears all prayers. When one begins a dialogue with God, God listens. God hears all communication directed to Him, and God doesn't listen to communication that is not directed to

Prayer is the opportunity to transcend the world in any given moment and connect with what is really True and Real.

Him. All of the chatter of the world goes ignored. It is just part of the dream. It isn't real. It has no meaning, and God doesn't listen to it.

When the mind split and the ego was invented, the Holy Spirit was the answer to that prayer and has been the answer to every prayer since. When one is afraid, they may pray for their physical safety, yet because this is a dream, what they really seek is the peace of knowing and remembering that this is just a dream and that there is nothing to fear. Every prayer is answered immediately, though when the answer is *received* is up to the one who prayed. The answer is given, and one will receive it when they are truly able and ready.

Candace: When I first started hearing God's Voice, It would come to me in meditation and throughout the day. Sometimes I would just put my attention on that Voice, and I would hear It. When DavidPaul sent me my first listener, I knew that I had to have a prayer to start the session with. I needed a way to call on this Voice and set an intention that what I heard would be this Voice and no other. So I asked God for a prayer, and though I still don't know exactly what it means, the prayer I heard was this:

"May it be with your blessings, God, that these words that come through are Yours, and only Yours. May they bring joy and light to those who hear them, and wisdom and knowledge to those who don't. Thank You, God. Amen."

Since that day, I've said this prayer every time I've shared this Voice. I also ask this Voice if It is willing to come through me. After more than fifteen years of asking, so far I've only heard three replies—"Yes," "Yes, of course," and "Yes, of course, precious one." I also ask this Voice if it will help me get out of the way of the communication, and sometimes I ask, "May this be exactly what we all need to hear," though I know this last request isn't necessary since we can only hear what we need to hear.

I usually say the prayer I was given three times in my head before I feel that I am connected with every word of it and connected with God and God's Voice. There have been times, however, when I've needed to say the prayer 20 or 30 times, and on a few rare occasions, when I've only said it once and felt connected. Sometimes I say the prayer out loud because I can't quiet my mind enough to connect with God. When I do, I often start off by saying hello to God and the Holy Spirit. Other times, I put my index finger on my forehead to help me focus as I say the prayer to myself. I also try to remember to thank God for the opportunity to hear His Voice before the session or after.

This prayer is important to me because it puts me in a clear place with a clear intention. I also find that saying hello to God and asking this Voice if It is willing to come through me feels like the right thing for me to do. Although I've come to understand that God's Voice loves to have the opportunity to share Truth with me, my family, and anyone else who seeks It, I will continue to ask if It is willing to come through me every time. As long as I keep hearing yes, I will keep sharing this Voice.

Each person will find their own way to connect with this Voice. For myself, I find that some sort of consistent ritual is helpful—it is something I can count on. When I have been away from the Voice for awhile and I say that prayer and reconnect, it is very familiar and comforting and can help erase the time that has gone by.

MANIFESTING IN THE WORLD

DavidPaul: There have been certain time periods in our lives when Candace and I have taken everything you can imagine to this Voice within us to receive assistance, including asking for new cars, homes, and promotions at work. We haven't always gotten what we've asked for. Can you talk with us about praying for things in the world? It seems like such a confusing topic sometimes.

The world is just a thought. If you say a prayer for something in the world, you are ultimately asking your mind to manifest what you prayed for. God doesn't create that for you. The Holy Spirit doesn't create that for you. These types of prayers are not answered in the sense that the clouds part and God brings down a house into the world for you. It is that you have the thought of something you want and based on your thoughts, you will either manifest that or you won't. When one prays for a relationship or a job, for example, they are really making an intention about what it is they want and then ultimately working with their mind to get it.

When one says a prayer for a relationship and then sits and waits for that relationship to show up, and they don't do anything but wait and keep asking God and wait some more and keep asking God, generally nothing happens. When one says a prayer for a relationship, they are declaring what they want and making an opening to move in that direction. They will then begin, with their mind, opening up to a relationship, contemplating what they want, and preparing themselves for it in a variety of ways. Again, based on their thinking, they will either manifest that relationship or they won't, and that has nothing to do with God. It is so easy to say, "God doesn't give me what I want. God doesn't answer my prayers," and to not take responsibility for what one manifests in the world.

God sees only your Perfection, only loves you unconditionally, and forever holds the Truth as what is Real. That has nothing to do with the world. It is not to say that it is pointless to pray for worldly things, only to be aware that the desire for prayer is ultimately the desire to connect with

God. Wanting something badly enough to pray for it is part of the design for you to be so motivated that you connect and communicate with God. You think you want these worldly things so badly that you will pray and ask God for them, but they are just the means, not the end.

Some people use prayer as proof that God loves them. Other people use prayer as proof that God does not. If one is able to manifest the big house that they prayed for, then God loves them, and if they are not able to manifest it, then God doesn't. This is obviously the ego's game because eventually there will be something that you pray for that will not manifest, and all of the other answered prayers will become meaningless.

If you want worldly things such as a family, a home, a job, good health, or anything else, you can ask God to join you in your thinking to manifest what is best for you. Ask God to join you in your thinking so that you can perceive the world, what's in it, and your path in such a way as to have whatever peace, connection, and comfort you desire. Ask the Holy Spirit to work with you and your mind to help you see the Truth of any situation so that you can know better what to ask for, how to ask for it, and how to move in that direction. Having worldly or earthly goals is not the problem. It is understanding how these goals manifest and your part in it that is confusing and can be invalidating or disruptive in your relationship with God.

ASK AND YOU SHALL RECEIVE

DavidPaul: I left Hawaii with two dreams in my heart: to fully embrace all that life had to offer and to find my life partner. What better way to do that, I thought, than to travel the world? So I purchased a one-way ticket around the globe with the hope

If you want worldly things such as a family, a home, a job, good health, or anything else, you can ask God to join you in your thinking to be able to manifest what is best for you.

of somehow returning the master of it. I thought to myself, "How difficult could it be to experience the world without judgment *and* find my life partner at the same time?"

About four months into my trip, I became obsessed with experiencing God as fully as possible. One morning, I found myself meditating in a cathedral in Thailand. I was on my hands and knees praying as deeply and fervently as possible for the willingness to experience God in every situation possible, no matter what it looked like. I remember that moment very clearly. It was almost as if I was praying to be given the most challenging situation imaginable ... somehow thinking that the opportunity to be so severely challenged would take me deeper in my experience of God. When my prayers were done, I opened my eyes and a man swiftly approached me. As he did, I remember thinking to myself, "This is my opportunity to acknowledge only God."

The man introduced himself as a school teacher, and we spent the entire day getting to know each other. Throughout the day, no matter what was said or done, I kept restoring my thoughts to only acknowledging God. To make a long story short, it turns out that this man was a con man, and by the end of the day, I had given him all of my money. There was one very surreal moment that I remember clearly to this day. I was about to hand over all my money when suddenly everything went into slow motion. In that moment, I heard a loud voice within my mind say, "I can't believe I'm doing this. I can't believe I'm doing this." And yet because I was so obsessed with experiencing God no matter what, I just handed over all my money and walked away. It wasn't until the next day that I realized I was never going to see that man again.

While I can't even begin to tell you about my adventure of making it back to the United States with only $50 left in my pocket, when I stepped off the plane in San Francisco three weeks later, I felt a bit disillusioned that I had not come back completely transformed or in any way more enlightened than when I had left. Living on my friend Felicia's couch in Oakland without a dime to my name, I became acutely aware that experiencing God in every situation and in every moment was not something I was going to check off of my to-do-list and be done with. It was going to be a moment-to-moment, day-to-day process that would unfold for the rest of my life.

With this new, sobering outlook on life, I set out to get a "real job" for the first time. I thought, if all things were truly equal, why not do what everyone else was doing in Silicon Valley? So I decided to get a job in high-tech. Within a few months, I landed a job doing tech-support, and in no time at all, I was back on my feet. I had an apartment, a car, and a whole new life. There was only one thing missing—someone to share it with.

As my life in the world began to stabilize, I came to the realization that the commitment I had made to my Self and God that morning in the Thai cathedral had opened me up to the understanding and perspective I needed to create a Holy Relationship with a life partner. Until that time, I had never really thought much about marriage, but as the months continued to tick by, my desire to create a Holy Relationship with someone began to grow stronger and stronger.

One night while I was sleeping, I had a dream that would change the course of my life. In the dream, I was kneeling down on a small boat in the middle of the ocean. Candace stood in front of me wearing a long, white dress. As I looked up at her, a wave of intense fear came over me. I could hardly breathe or speak. I struggled to open my mouth, and as I did, I suddenly woke up.

Completely stunned, I immediately sat up in bed, closed my eyes, and visualized being back in the dream. I felt the fear that had gripped me so strongly, and as it began to melt away, a deep and abiding love for Candace flowed into me, a love for her that I had never felt before. I spent several hours in meditation that night, joining with and feeling all of the thoughts and emotions that arose within me. I also sought guidance on what was in my highest good and how to deal with this new experience. By the time I was done, I knew that I loved Candace and wanted to have a life with her. There was only one problem—she was committed to someone else!

I agonized for days whether I should tell her. In the end, I realized that I only wanted her to be happy and did not want to ruin what she was making for herself, so I said, "God, if this is meant to be, it's in Your Hands. There's nothing I can do." I then took down her picture at work and stopped calling or e-mailing her.

Six months later, she called to say that she was leaving her boyfriend. My heart leapt, and my adrenaline surged. I broke out in a sweat. Six phone calls, six weeks, and one plane ticket later, she was on her way to California to begin a life with me. It is only now after eleven years of marriage and eight years of parenting that I can half-jokingly say that the answer to my prayer of wanting to experience God under all circumstances was not answered by being left destitute half way around the world with no way to get home. Marriage and parenthood have given me far more opportunities for growth and enlightenment than anything else I could have ever dreamed up!

FOR THE HIGHEST GOOD OF ALL

Candace: When DavidPaul and I first began seeking guidance and direction from this Voice within us, we had very little framework or perspective about prayer. We blurted out whatever question we had on our minds, and we asked for insight and communication on just about everything we wanted in our lives. Over time, this Voice began to teach us more about prayer and how to use it to receive what we truly wanted. Eventually, we were taught about the concept of asking for what was in our highest good. Because this approach to prayer has had such a

In praying for the highest good in any situation, you can trust that whatever is truly the best for one's path will unfold.

profound impact upon us, "God, can You explain what it means to ask for what is in one's highest good when seeking guidance, direction, or in prayer?"

When one is aware that they do not know what is the best outcome, when they do not know what is best for someone else or themselves, or when they do not know how something should unfold, though they may have beliefs or thoughts of how they would like it to unfold, one can simply pray for that which is in the highest good. In praying for the highest good in any situation, you can trust that whatever is truly the best for one's path will unfold. This can include a situation involving a loved one or your family, or it could be about a war in another part of the world.

Pray for that which is in the highest good of everyone involved and ask God to be with everyone in their thinking, so that if they choose, they may be able to perceive Right-Mindedness for a moment. The pattern in the world is to seek the path of least resistance. It is the norm for one to do that which is easiest, with the quickest results or most immediate gratification. Most advice and solutions offer short-term answers, rather than a long-term answers. When one asks for guidance involving a particular situation and asks for that which is in their highest good, what they receive may not necessarily be the easiest, quickest, or most immediately gratifying answer, but rather may be a long-term solution.

For example, when two people are in a relationship with one another and one person no longer wants to be in the relationship, the one who wants to continue the relationship may feel heart-broken and think that the simplest solution would be to convince the other person, who is already in their life, to stay in the relationship so they will not have to feel pain, sadness, or loneliness.

If one were in that situation and praying for guidance and

asking for that which is in their highest good, they may hear why it is that they have been with that person, what it is they have been learning, what they have gained from that experience, and why now it is important to let it go. They may hear that ultimately there is a better situation for them at hand and that the relationship they are in has already fulfilled its purpose. It is complete for whatever reason. Just because someone does not feel complete with a situation has nothing to do with what is in their highest good. If they ask what is in their highest good, they may hear it is time to let this relationship go, bless it for all the ways it has served them, seek to find peace with this person in their heart, and have faith knowing that a better situation is ahead. They can trust and make peace with what is happening and move on.

For most, this proposition seems painful, difficult, lonely, and scary. They might think that the short-term solution of trying to convince their partner to stay is safer, happier, less scary, and less lonely. When you look at the two options, you can see that seeking peace and having faith are the only ways to go, and yet in the moment, one might try to convince the other to stay in order to avoid their pain. What they do not realize is how much pain they are already in at that moment. When one stops to acknowledge how much pain they are really in because of their fears, they would choose peace. Instead, what one has is the illusion that hope brings them in a short-term solution.

In asking for that which is in one's highest good, it is important to acknowledge that one does not know what is in their highest good. It is easy to think one knows, and yet the Truth of that is different indeed. You come to trust and understand what is in your highest good by putting things in God's Hands. It is easy to look at different options and think you know what is best, but what is truly in the highest good means that which may offer you the most learning, the most

When you pray for yourself, you are ultimately praying for all. When you pray for another, you are ultimately praying for yourself.

growth, the most evolution, the right opportunity to move in the direction that you are ultimately seeking or the one that will uncover for you something you need. One cannot see into the future and know what would be best for them, and yet, in asking for that which is in your highest good, the universe will conspire to bring you toward it by knowing all things.

You cannot make a mistake, and at the same time, there are opportunities, directions, and relationships that would give you everything if you are willing. Other opportunities will support you in the status quo and do not offer you that push to move in the direction that you are ultimately seeking. Oftentimes, you need a little shove to get there.

PRAYING FOR OTHER PEOPLE

DavidPaul: If I can't know what's in *my* highest good, I'm guessing I can't know what is in another person's highest good either then, right?

That's correct.

DavidPaul: So how do we pray for other people?

Ultimately, every prayer is for the Whole, for the Sonship, for God's Child. When you pray for yourself, you are ultimately praying for all. When you pray for another, you are ultimately praying for yourself. If you say a prayer for someone else, you are giving the gift of that prayer to all of God's Children because your instant of remembering God, venturing into Truth, and being in Reality is the gift you give to the Whole when you do it. Every moment that each perceived child of God experiences Truth is a moment that everyone can have that Truth.

God does not answer worldly prayers in the way you might perceive. If you say a prayer asking for someone's health, God will not address the issue of this person's health. It will be up to that person and their mind to perceive their health differently. If it is that person's path to have a certain disease and struggle with that experience and learn and grow as a result of that, then they will continue to move along on that path. This is not conscious often times and one may be fighting their illness, but it is not something that you can change within their mind; only they can change that within their mind.

When you say a prayer for someone's health, you can be aware that you are ultimately praying for your own health and allow yourself to become more aware of how your thinking is impacting your health. When you change your thinking about your health, you open the door for another to see that it is possible to change their thinking and that may be the biggest gift you can offer to the one you are praying for. Even if one sees that it is possible to affect their health with their thinking, they may still choose not to and that is their path.

If you really want to pray for someone else, you can say, "God, if it be in this person's highest good, would You help to reassure them that You are with them always, that they are loved, and that they are whole and safe in Your Arms?" Then you can know that this prayer will be answered, because it is already done.

PRAYING FOR UNDERSTANDING

Candace: What about when things aren't going as we would like them to? What would be a good thing to pray for in those situations?

If your life is unfolding differently than you hoped or your life is devastating in some way, rather than pray for it to be different or pray for how you think you want your life to be, it is important to pray for understanding. Herein lies the key to happiness.

Pray for the peace that can come to you from understanding what is happening, why it is happening, and how it can ultimately serve you. It is easy to mourn a loss, no matter what that is—a person, a place, or a thing. It is easy to fear a change. It is easy to begrudge a difference and blame God, when one could instead have faith that what is unfolding must be in their highest good and ask God for the understanding to go with that loss or change.

In seeking understanding, you can experience your life in such a way that it is more of a free fall rather than a derailed train. It is the same life—the free fall or the derailed train—in one, there is faith and understanding, and in the other, there is blame and devastation. When you pray for peace and understanding, you will always have that prayer answered.

SIMPLIFYING PRAYER

DavidPaul: Prayer can sometimes seem so complicated. What would be a simple way to pray?

Prayer is talking to God, and that can take any form imaginable. The simplest, most truthful, and most profound prayer would be, "Thank you." "Thank You, God, for everything You have given me," while understanding that the majority of the gifts that God has given you have yet to be received in the sense of being understood or acknowledged. Though prayer is not necessary in Truth—because everything has already been given to you—when you have the idea that you are separate from God and live in the world, struggling, suffering, and

✦

In seeking understanding, you can experience your life in such a way that it is more of a free fall rather than a derailed train. It is the same life—the free fall or the derailed train—in one, there is faith and understanding, and in the other, there is blame and devastation. When you pray for peace and understanding, you will always have that prayer answered.

doing without, prayer seems necessary indeed.

If you are praying for what you know to be true, instead of asking for it, you can just give thanks for it. If you want to ask for what is in the highest good of two warring groups, for example, and you want to ask God to join them in their Right-Thinking, you can say, "Thank You, God, for the ever presence of Truth within the minds of all of God's Children so that we may know what is best in every moment," or something similar that acknowledges what is Real and True *already.*

If you want to hear God, instead of saying, "Please God, I want to hear your Voice in all that I do," you can say instead, "God, thank You for giving me your Voice that I may hear You in every moment that I choose. God, thank you for the opportunity of Right-Thinking in any moment." In this way, you acknowledge and validate what really *is* rather than the thought of needing something, or wanting something, as if God would allow His Children to go out into the world without all of their needs met. It is not possible. Your needs have already been met. Your prayer has been answered, and God's Voice has been given to you to choose in any and every moment so you may have peace, love, and remembrance of the Truth of who you are. "Thank you, God, for the Peace, Love, and Joy that I have." You can say that prayer regardless of how you are feeling because, in Truth, you have been given Peace, Love, and Joy, and that is the Truth of who and what you are. It is only a thought that keeps you from It.

The more that you acknowledge and validate the Truth, the more you will experience Truth in the world. "Thank you, God, for putting Your Voice into each perceived Child of God in the world so that I have the unending opportunity to hear your Voice in everyone I encounter. Thank you, God, for my true safety. Thank you that I need never fear because in Truth, I am always at Home with You." When you have the thought of needing or wanting something that is Right-Minded, you can remember that you do have it. Give thanks for it, and you will start to bring it more into your awareness, experience, and belief.

God does not perceive the world because God only has full knowledge of Truth and there is no opposite to that. There are no lies. There are no illusions. There is no hate in opposition to God's Love or any other opposite you can think of. There is only Truth and the knowledge of that Truth; therefore, God cannot perceive the world or any of your needs in the world.

God gave you the Holy Spirit to be able to perceive the illusion with you to help you get to the other side. If the Holy Spirit were not willing to perceive the illusion, the Holy Spirit would not be able to help you out of it. When you have a situation in the world that causes you pain or suffering, you can pray to the Holy Spirit to change your thinking about the situation. The Holy Spirit can then either remind you that this is all a dream or give you a perspective of Truth that allows you to have peace because you understand why what appears to be happening is happening. Your body, your family, your home, your job, where you live, and the rest of the world are all a dream.

Eventually, your prayers can become very comfortable, fluid, loving, and warm. They can be an easy back and forth dialogue that includes acknowledging God, giving thanks, and feeling God's Presence within your heart and mind, giving you a sense of overall connectedness with God. Prayer opens the door and God is waiting patiently on the other side of that door, at all times, in all situations, to join with you. Prayer is an experience, not a request. It is a joining, not a wanting. Prayer is an opening and a gift. Prayer is the gift itself rather than what it is you are praying for. Prayer is the answer to the prayer.

DavidPaul: How we came to write this book illustrates the power of using prayer in its simplest form. In 1999, I had the opportunity to work for America Online (AOL). Although I was excited to work at such a fast-growing Internet company and dreamed of making millions in stock options, I knew in my heart that I did not want a career in corporate America and that our life's work involved sharing God's Voice with others. Although this was true, we were not ready to pursue that dream yet. We were just starting a family and thought we needed a good paying job to support ourselves in the high-priced Silicon Valley, so I took the job with one caveat—I would only commit to corporate life for four years—no matter what.

Before we knew it, the Internet bubble had burst, and three years later, our AOL stock options were worthless, literally not worth a dime. We were living month-to-month with little money in savings, and my job, with all of the downsizing and layoffs at AOL, was only becoming more difficult and stressful.

Around this time, we received guidance to make a list of the most important things in our lives and to use that list to establish a family prayer. We were guided to write this prayer as if it were already true, as though we had already received all that we were asking for and wanting. We thought about our goals for quite awhile and then wrote the following prayer:

"Thank You, God, that we are a happy, healthy, three-parent family, living our soul purpose in union with the Holy Spirit, while being financially provided for in every way." (For us, the term three-parent family acknowledged that God was our daughter's true Parent, as well as ours.)

We were guided to say this prayer as often as possible throughout the day. Even though it was difficult at times to force this reality upon our minds when we were not feeling happy, healthy, or financially provided for, saying the prayer helped us to literally form this reality within our minds.

Practically to the day of my four year anniversary at AOL, with my stock options fully vested and still worthless, my hands started hurting. With each passing day, they became worse and worse. Soon, I could no longer type, and it was becoming very

P rayer is talking to God and that can take any form imaginable. The simplest, most truthful, and most profound prayer would be, "Thank you."

difficult to do my job. Before I knew it, my career at AOL started going down the drain. In our quest to find a cure for my hands, we did a lot of soul searching and checked in with the Holy Spirit regularly. Eventually, we came to view my disability as an opportunity to change the course of our lives.

Around this time, Candace and our daughter went to visit Candace's father who was living on eleven acres in Oregon. While Candace was there, she fell in love with being on the land and watching our daughter freely come and go from her father's rural house.

Back at AOL, the fear, control, and uncertainty within the company was at an all-time high. Management was talking of impending layoffs, and it had been rumored that my position was among them. After checking in with this Voice, we decided to put our townhouse on the market so we wouldn't be burdened with a house payment if I lost my job. The following day, our next door neighbors, who were renting their unit, said they were interested in buying our townhouse, which meant no realtor fees or open houses. We jumped at the chance.

We immediately called Candace's father and asked if we could live in the cabin on his property, and because his tenants had unexpectedly vacated only weeks before, he excitedly said yes. One week later, I was laid off from work. Three weeks later, escrow closed on our townhouse, and that day we moved to Oregon. If we liquidated all of our assets and lived simply, we would have enough money to last us possibly two years, which would be enough time to follow our dream of writing this book.

One month after selling our townhouse and moving to Oregon, we found a wonderful preschool for our daughter three mornings a week, and with no corporate job keeping us busy, we began writing *The Voice for Love*. In so doing, we truly fulfilled our dream of being a happy, healthy, three-parent family, living our soul purpose in union with the Holy Spirit, while being financially provided for in every way. And we have

God and the Holy Spirit to thank for guiding and supporting us every step of the way.

✧ EXERCISE – AN OPPORTUNITY TO CONNECT

Set aside a certain time each day for prayer. This need only be a few minutes or it can be as long as you like, but have a certain time every day that you set aside to connect with God. This might be the first thing you do in the morning, the last thing you do at night, something you do every day during your lunch break, or at any other time during the day. Regardless, do try to give yourself a consistent moment that you reserve for this connection.

If you decide to use the first minutes of your waking for prayer, then as you begin to come out of your sleep, remind yourself that this is your prayer time and begin to prepare yourself for that. You might continue lying down. You may decide to sit up. You may have your eyes open or closed, or have your arms and legs in a certain position. It only matters what is comfortable or meaningful for you. It can be helpful to have some sort of ritual where you use the same sort of process or behavior each time.

In addition, remind yourself that prayer is not asking God for something, but rather the opportunity to connect with God and open the door to God. The door is always there and from God's side, it is always open, so the intent to pray in this way allows the door to open on your side as well.

Begin to focus on God. You might say, "Hello," or "Good morning, God, it's me," or any type of dialogue you like. You may want to give thanks for your rest and the new day. You may want to share something that is in your heart and mind to share. You may want to ask a question, or you may want to complain about a situation. Regardless, do so with the intent, first and foremost, to connect with God, to connect with this loving Friend, Parent, and Companion.

You can then rest from your communication and imagine, if you like, hearing what God has to say back to you. God's Voice within you will deliver the Messages directly to you, swiftly and with love, if you listen. You may experience a sense of peace or gratitude or some insight or awareness about a situation. You may perceive something differently. It does not matter, just that you use this time with the intent to connect, join, and share with God.

Give thanks for your joining, and when you are complete, go about your day while doing the best you can to be mindful of the experience you just had. You may want to consider beginning and ending your day in this way. Of course, you are welcome to join with God as often as possible, as often as you like, or as often as it occurs to you. God is always waiting patiently for you to open that door.

CHAPTER SUMMARY

Prayer is the opportunity to join with our Creator, with the Presence of Love that God is. Prayer is our decision to see things differently and to connect with the part of our Self that *is* God's Voice in the world. Because we are the ones who make things happen in the world through our own thinking—through the creative power of our mind—it is not necessary to pray to God to help us manifest what we want in the world. When we do, we are really just working with our own mind to create what it is we truly want.

If we wish to have peace and faith *while* we create in the world, praying for the highest good of all to unfold can be very helpful because it helps us acknowledge that we cannot know what is best for us or anyone else, and it helps us trust that whatever *is* happening must surely be what is best for all.

Ultimately, prayer is the opportunity to connect with God and to acknowledge what already *is*. It is the opportunity to recognize the Truth, that all that we truly seek has already been given us and that we remain as God created us to be. When we give thanks for what already *is*, we magnetize to us even more of *It*. With this perspective, gratitude is the simplest form of prayer there is.

– 10 –

Quieting Your Mind

*When one quiets the mind, they create an
invitation to God to join with them.*

I t can be difficult to hear God's Voice over the noise of
the world because the noise and the world seem to
be outside of you. There is a place you can go where the
world does not exist, and that is within. When you go
within, you leave the world and step into a quiet place
where God can enter. God does not enter the world,
so God's pathway to you is through Right-Mindedness
and the Holy Spirit. By going within, quieting the mind,
and inviting God to join you in this place of Truth, you
cannot help but hear God's Voice. It is all that is left in
the quietness.

SETTING THE STAGE

DavidPaul: While it is not necessary to meditate in the formal
sense to access our Inner Wisdom, closing our eyes and going
within has played a significant role for us personally in coming

It is through meditation that one
sets the stage for listening to God.
Part of that preparation involves
making a date with God, just as you
would with anyone you wanted to
engage in relationship with.

to hear God's Voice within us, as well as accessing this Voice on an ongoing basis.

It is through meditation that one sets the stage for listening to God. Part of that preparation involves making a date with God, just as you would with anyone you wanted to engage in relationship with. If one really wanted to be married and have a family, for example, they would likely have as their priority clearing their calendar, meeting people, setting up dates, making reservations, getting tickets, dressing up, brushing their teeth, going on dates and everything else they need to do to truly connect with someone. They do this over and over and over again until eventually they make a connection with someone who they want to have a life with. It is the same in your relationship with God. If you want to have a lifelong partnership with God, then you court God. You set up the date, the time, the place, the reservations, the tickets, and whatever else that looks like metaphorically, so you can honor that time and give it the value that it truly has. You would approach meditation in the same way. It is a very revered time that one would establish with God on a regular basis.

Meditation dims the chatter of the world and the voice of the ego so that you can more easily join with God and hear the Voice of Truth within you. You do this physically by first finding a quiet place to sit and be still, turning off the ringers on your phones, putting a *Do Not Disturb* sign on your door, or anything else you need to do to close yourself off from the world so you can have your date with God.

Generally speaking, it is important to sit upright rather than lie down in meditation. For nearly everyone, if you lie down to meditate, you will fall asleep. That is called a nap, not meditation. If you are so tired that sitting there is impossible, you can either get up and move around and attempt to re-energize yourself and then sit back down, or you can lie down and rest for little bit and then sit back up and try again. If you need to rest, try to give yourself enough time to meditate after your rest so that it doesn't turn into just a nap. You may find that after some rest it becomes very simple to focus in meditation.

One may also find a particular sitting position to be more comfortable than another. In general, it's good to sit in a chair and have your feet on the floor to help you be more awake and present. If you are comfortable sitting on the floor or on a cushion with your legs crossed lotus style, of course, that is fine as well. For some, there is effort in sitting this way and in holding their back up. They often become more focused on that than on allowing their mind to become emptied and open for a connection with God. There are no rules; just find a position that truly serves you.

If you have a situation that is weighing heavily on your mind or distracting you in your meditation and you cannot overcome it, you can ask God's Voice to be with you and to help restore you to Right-Thinking in that particular situation so that you can have your peace and your connectedness with God. You can ask this Inner Voice for a perspective on that situation that allows you to understand your part in it, or to accept what you think you may have done, or to accept or understand what you think another may have done. Eventually you may come to understand that none of those things actually happened. It was only the way your mind perceived them and now your mind is free again to connect with God. These encounters and situations are fabricated by the ego as very efficient and effective distractions from God. Once you have peace with something, your mind is then free to connect with Truth once again.

CREATING A PRACTICE

It seems simple to say that prayer is talking to God and meditation is listening to God, but that is truly the case. If you want to connect with God, you can begin the conversation with prayer and you can listen to the response that God has for you through the practice of meditation because God's Voice exists in the quietness of your Right-Mind. To attain this connection or engage in this conversation, you have to go to where the other party is, and that is not in the loudness and the chaos of the world but in the quietness of your Right-Mind. To go there requires a practice, and that practice would be any form of meditation that restores you to your Right-Mind so that you can go where God is, where God's Voice is, and join Him there.

Certainly, you are One with God and that has never changed. Yet from your perspective that the world is real and that you are separate, accessing your Inner Voice is the most efficient way to be restored to God in your awareness, and the practice of meditation is what can take you there. Of course one can become very desperate, pleading, begging, despondent, on their knees, and they may seek and find God in that moment and that may serve them perfectly, but one would not want to have to be desperate and pleading and on their knees every day to connect with God. It would be so much kinder to sit quietly in a room with the door closed and attempt to focus inward and get to a place of Right-Mindedness so you can have an ongoing relationship with God through a practice that is effortless, nurturing, and fulfilling beyond your wildest dreams, and you can spare your knees at the same time!

Whenever you have a thought that causes you pain, makes you sad, frustrated, angry, disappointed, depressed, or longing, you can seek Right-Mindedness in whatever way might be right for you. You can ask, "Is that thought true?" or you may take a break, sit down, breathe, and ask to be restored to Right-Mindedness. You may ask this Voice to be with you and help you to overcome those thoughts so that you can see the Truth of the situation. The more that you have a meditation practice in your life, the easier it will be for you to return to that practice in your time of need. It is through this practice that you will connect with the only thing that can really help you, and that is the most wonderful gift you can give yourself and all of God's Children.

✧ EXERCISES – QUIETING THE MIND

The purpose of meditation is to focus your mind in such a way that you no longer hear the voice of the ego and can instead join with God, God's Voice, Truth, Source, Peace, Joy, or whatever it is you are seeking. Before reading the following exercises, it's important to acknowledge and validate what you are already doing to quiet your mind.

If you don't have a meditation practice, take some time to think about what methods or practices have worked for you in the past. Chances are you have done something that has allowed you to experience your connection with Source. You may have read a specific book, taken a vacation by yourself, said a particular prayer or mantra, hiked to a beautiful place, or done any number of things that assisted you in feeling connected.

The exercises below are an option for those who do not have a regular meditation practice or for those looking to explore other methods. They are not intended to be all encompassing or definitive. If you presently have a practice that helps you quiet your mind, by all means continue to use it. The possibilities for quieting the mind are truly unlimited.

I t seems simple to say that prayer
is talking to God and meditation is
listening to God, but that is
truly the case.

VISUALIZATION

Many people enjoy using visualization to connect with God. Visualization can help focus the mind on Truth. Any visualization that serves this purpose may be used. Below are a few options. Practice the ones that call to you.

1. BULLDOZING THE MIND

With your eyes closed, imagine your mind as a lush and beautiful garden that has not been tended to in some time. The flowers may have shriveled up. The delicious fruit might have fallen to the ground and become rotten. The soil may have dried up or weeds may have taken over.

Now imagine that there is a large bulldozer in front of you. Use this bulldozer to break up the dry and hardened soil. Use it to turn the rocky earth. As you do, the rich soil that has always been there soon rises to the surface. Continue to turn the soil over and over until you see that the earth has become soft, moist, and fertile once again. This may take a little time.

When the soil is ready, ask God for new seeds to plant. Place them in the rich, fertile soil and then water them. Tend them and give them plenty of sunshine. Eventually, new life begins to sprout and grow. Before long, your garden is lush and beautiful once again.

Note: This visualization may take you thirty minutes or it may take you two months. In either case, visualizing a barren garden does not make it true nor does it mean that you will not hear this Inner Voice until your garden is bursting with life. It is only to say that you can visualize breaking up the parts of your mind that are not fully receptive to hearing God's Voice. With this intention, this visualization may begin to open your mind to receiving God's Voice in new or different ways.

2. A Bridge to the Mind of God

Since this Voice within you is the Bridge to the Mind of God, close your eyes and envision that you are standing on one side of a bridge and God's Mind is on the other side of the bridge. This bridge can look any way you like. It might cross over water. It could be a heavenly structure extending from one cloud to another with nothing below it. It may be an image of a rainbow—whatever comes to you as you close your eyes and go within is perfect.

Imagine yourself walking up to that bridge, making a decision to cross it, and then moving across that bridge until you are half way across it. This is where you can release any thoughts of the ego from your mind to be cleansed and transformed into Right-Minded thoughts. You can release judgment, sadness, envy, guilt, anger, or any other emotions you no longer want. They will all be washed away and transformed.

When you are ready, continue crossing the bridge until you reach the other side. This is the Mind of God. This is where all are One. You have now entered into a sacred place within yourself where you can access all Truths. It is familiar territory to you. Setting an intention to go there when you want to communicate with God's Voice will bring clarity to the experience.

3. Your Meeting Place with God

Imagine a meeting place where you and God join together to connect and communicate. This is a place where you can step out of the world and rendezvous with God, a place where you know God is waiting for you. It can be as beautiful, as simple, or as sweet or mundane a place as you desire. Knowing that

The purpose of meditation is to focus your mind in such a way that you no longer hear the voice of the ego and can instead join with God, God's Voice, Truth, Source, Peace, Joy, or whatever it is you are seeking.

God is joining you there, chances are it will be special.

It might be a place that you dream of being. It may be surrounded by mountains, or water, or something that allows it to be a place that is only entered by you, God, and God's Voice. Over time, having a consistent image related to joining with God can make it easier and easier to get there, to be there, and to join with God in this way. This is not a place that is outside of you. It is a place that is within you where God is always waiting to join with you.

4. GOLDEN LIGHT

With your eyes closed, visualize someone standing in front of you. This could be someone you know or don't know, someone you care about, or someone you have an issue with. As you gaze upon them, you see a golden light beginning to spin around them like a long piece of yarn. The light slowly continues to circle around their body, and as it does, it begins to form a ball of golden light around them. The light continues around and around until it eventually becomes completely solid.

When there are no holes or gaps in the ball of light and it is completely surrounding the person in front of you, imagine that the ball of light begins to radiate infinitely inward toward their body, filling every cell of their body along the way. When this inward journey is complete, imagine that the ball of light begins to radiate outward, beyond the boundaries of the universe and into infinity. Soon, all that exists is golden light and a thin outline of the person standing in front of you.

This vision is symbolic of the Truth of who they are. As you gaze upon their essence, speak these or other words of Truth to them, "I give you the Peace of God. Accept It, for this *is* who you are, and you are blessed above all things."

5. Breathing

For some, conscious breathing is a technique that can help the mind become focused on one thing. Focusing on the breath can help one to slow down and go within.

There are a variety of methods one can use. You may sit down and begin to take deep breaths in and out, in and out, focusing on your breath exclusively. While you are doing that, you may also use some sort of mantra. For example, you may hold one thought as you breathe in and another as you breathe out. You may breathe in and say silently to yourself, "I am," and you may breathe out saying silently to yourself, "at peace," or "loved," or "connected with God," or any statement that feels right to you.

You may want to breathe in through your nose and out through your mouth, or vice versa; or you may prefer breathing in and out through only your nose. You might want to use a form of yogic breath work where your mouth is closed and yet you hear your breathing within your esophagus. Or, you might breathe in for a certain count—1, 2, 3, 4, then hold your breath 1, 2, 3, 4, then breathe out 1, 2, 3, 4—so that all of the counts are the same, continuing to do this until there is a natural rhythm.

It does not matter which technique you follow. Do what is easy and natural for you so that you can focus inwardly rather than thinking about your day, the dishes, your mate, or what food you are going to make for a party on Saturday. Concentrating on your breath allows you to focus on the here and now. Breathe in whatever way allows you to be comfortable, relaxed, or get into a meditative state, and allow this focus on the breath to keep you from the distractions of the mind. As you focus on your breath, you can oftentimes be transported to a meditative state where you are seemingly beyond the world. You may find after just breathing consciously for a period of time that the world has fallen away and that you have become very still and quiet within.

6. Sound and Mantras

You may close your eyes and not focus on your breathing but focus instead on a particular sound. In some cultures, it would be the sound of *Om* or *Huu* or something similar. Making these sounds aloud or in your mind helps to quiet the mind, leaving it open for communion with God.

If you don't have a specific sound in mind, you might have a statement, mantra, invitation, or prayer that you say over and over again—"I am one with God," or "I am at peace," or "Everything is perfect," or "I am as God created me," or any statement or thought that serves you. Repeat that thought over and over again in your mind, allowing that thought to become true for you in your thinking. Saying something over and over again or listening to something repeatedly in meditation or throughout your day helps your mind stay focused on thoughts that serve you.

You may prefer to practice this while taking a walk. (This would not include walking with someone else or in a group.) As you walk, you might hold one thought with one step and a different thought with the next—with your first step, "I am," and with your next step, "with God," and so on as you walk; or you might say a prayer over and over again as you walk. How you meditate while walking is irrelevant if it serves you in your goal of connecting with or hearing God's Voice.

7. Silence

You may have periods of time that you set aside to *not* communicate. You may have hours or days of silence. You may set aside one period of time each week where you do not communicate out loud. This is a quiet and reflective time. You can let those around you know that you will not be communicating during that time. Let the phone and the door go unanswered and listen instead to Who is calling you within.

If you are having periods of time in your life that are silent, as they become more reflective, the mind begins to quiet. Your whole inside begins to quiet, and this creates the opportunity to hear that which has always been there—God's Voice. This Voice for Peace does not shout over all the noise of the world, but rather waits for a quiet opening to make Its Presence known.

8. Feeling

One way to connect with God is to simply sit and feel His Presence, feel His Love, feel His Grace surrounding you, within you. You may envision yourself in God's Arms or with God wrapped around you like a blanket. You might be sitting in the palm of God's Hand, safe and secure. Use whatever concept allows you to experience being cared for, loved, or watched over by God, and then allow yourself to experience what it feels like to just feel God's Love and Presence. You can feel it in you, around you, and through you. Focus on that feeling. Wallow in that feeling. Allow yourself to go as deep into that feeling as you can. You may laugh. You may cry. You may be very, very quiet and still. You may experience all those things in the process of feeling God.

God is always ready to join with you, and as you set your intention and focus on connecting in this way, you cannot help but experience this joining. When you allow yourself to experience how it feels when you are so completely filled and overflowing with the sensation of God that you think you might burst, you give yourself an inkling of what your true relationship with God really is.

9. EXTENDING LOVE

When one goes within, closes their eyes, and begins to become aware of the thoughts they are thinking, the emotions they are feeling, and the beliefs and judgments that they have, one can learn to relate to those thoughts in such a way that the thoughts no longer have any power over them. When one befriends a thought, in any form that that thought may take, one is extending love, kindness, and understanding to that thought. In that moment, the one who is extending this love is not believing that thought, judging that thought, suppressing that thought, or giving that thought any meaning, power, or reality. They are using that thought as an opportunity to extend love. When one "befriends their thoughts" in this way, they are being the presence of the Holy Spirit, acknowledging what appears to be arising within the mind yet only extending Love. In so doing, one sees the thought for what it is, and the thought merely falls away, dissolving in the Light of the perfect Love that God is.

CHAPTER SUMMARY

Meditation is a state of mind that allows us to experience our connection with God, Truth, and this Voice for Love within us. It is a state of being that is receptive, calm, and non-attached to whatever is happening around us or within us. While it is certainly possible to experience this state of mind spontaneously without our conscious involvement, if we want to intentionally deepen our experience of this Voice within us and more fully integrate this Voice into our lives, it is helpful to establish a meditation practice that we can use to consistently access this quiet place within.

Meditation does not have to be difficult or time consuming. With practice, it can take just a few moments to quiet the mind and join with God in our awareness. When we are familiar and comfortable with our experience of this Presence of Love within us through a regular practice of going within, receiving guidance and communication while still interacting in the world becomes as natural and easy as connecting with a close friend.

– 11 –

Accessing Your Inner Voice

Every time you hear a loving thought or speak a loving word, you are hearing God's Voice.

Hearing God's Voice is everything you have longed for, everything you have dreamed of, and what you have been convinced is impossible. Hearing God's Voice nourishes you in a way that you could never be nourished in the world. Hearing this Voice is an experience that cannot be contained within the body. It is different than you might imagine because it is not of this world. When you hear this Voice, you transcend the world in that moment. This Voice restores you to all that is True and Real and also guides and directs you in what is not real so that you can notice the difference and eventually leave the world behind.

PREREQUISITES FOR HEARING YOUR INNER VOICE

DavidPaul: There are so many ways to hear God's Voice in the world. Are there any actual prerequisites for hearing this Voice in our lives?

All that one needs in order to hear God's Voice is the desire. If the desire is there, the Voice will be heard. If you desire to hear God's Voice, then you will and that is the beginning and the end of that. How you get there is another matter. How you get to the place of having desire is each one's fate. The desire is there for everyone. It is just a matter of remembering it.

For some, the desire is so strong that nothing else is sought over a lifetime. For others, it is forgotten completely, and yet the same desire is within each one. If you seek to hear God, you will—in all ways, in all things, through all means—and it is up to you to recognize and receive the Messages. You can hear God in everything—in the silence, in the chaos, in conversations over the phone, in a book, and in so many other ways. If you are open and willing to allow God's Voice to take any form through your trust and your faith, by desiring to hear God, you will.

If you desire to hear God, all around you is God speaking, but if you do not like the delivery or you do not value the delivery, God's Voice won't be received. It is important to not be attached to a certain delivery but rather be open to all things. If you desire to hear God's Voice within your heart and mind, then hold a very clear intention for that to unfold in your life, and be clear that you are willing to make whatever seeming sacrifices are needed. This is said tongue-in-cheek because the sacrifices one makes to hear God's Voice are so meaningless and yet can seem like everything. You may lose that which you think you value. You may lose that which you think is important to you. You may lose that which you think matters to you in the process of hearing God's Voice because you have been convinced by the ego that everything you see is real, that everything you have matters, and that everything you want is important. Once you hear God's Voice, the ego falls away in that instant. You can only hear one or the other. It is not possible for them to speak over each other.

As you open to hearing God's Voice, the ego will become quiet for that moment and all that you seem to value in the world will fall away; all that you value will become meaningless and that which is True will rest in your heart and your mind—Heaven. In that moment, you will be in Heaven and the world will be gone.

You must be willing to give up all that you seem to be attached to now in order to hear Truth, because Truth does not involve anything in the world. Hearing Truth can feel like a very humbling experience because you are so used to being right, being the best, or being first. In the presence of Truth, none of that exists. You have to be willing to no longer be the best at this, first at that, or have your identity be associated with something in the world. The Truth is that you are a Child of God, complete, whole, and loved as you are, just because you are, which has nothing to do with what you do in the world, how you do it, who you do it with, or anything else.

For some, the risk of giving up all that is familiar, known, comfortable, rewarding, validating, and esteeming is too high a price to pay to hear God's Voice, and yet you cannot forget that what you desire is to know the Truth.

DavidPaul: Experiencing the Truth of who I am while reading a transcript from Jesus and literally being brought back to life in Hawaii by the Holy Spirit, it's easy to see why I would be so motivated to hear God's Voice. As a result of these experiences, a deep desire to have and use this Resource for myself began to grow within me.

All that one needs in order to hear God's Voice is the desire. If the desire is there, the Voice will be heard.

I first felt it in Hawaii. It deepened throughout my travels around the world, and it blossomed into an irresistible passion upon my return to the mainland. I practiced and practiced, tried and tried, and surrendered with all my might to hear this Voice within me, but no matter what I did, I just couldn't hear It. I'd meditate for hours, reach a place of complete silence and peace within me, surrender and listen in every way I could imagine, but no matter how hard I tried or didn't try, it was always the same—I'd eventually give up in frustration, disappointment, and sometimes anger.

Over the course of several years, I probably prayed to hear God's Voice within me at least a thousand times. I asked friends and mentors how they did it, and did everything they told me to do—every exercise, every meditation, every prayer, but nothing seemed to help. My passion, commitment, and drive to hear and open to this Voice would grow with every exercise I was given, but I would quickly tumble into depression, anger, and hopelessness after weeks or months of trying with no success. This was so frustrating and devastating that I would sometimes cry in defeat. Eventually, after several years of struggle, I finally gave up. While a part of me felt like a failure, another part of me felt relieved to give up the fight. I made a commitment to stop trying to hear God's Voice within me, and it felt good.

When Candace and I became a couple a few years later, we started checking in with God's Voice on a regular basis. Shortly thereafter, my desire and passion to hear this Voice with me was rekindled and I began to ask this Voice through Candace for guidance on how to open up to hearing God's Voice for myself. Because of my past history of trying to hear this Voice within me with no apparent success, the guidance I received through Candace was to *not seek* this Voice within me, but instead to ask for external signs in the world in response to my questions.

So before getting out of bed each morning, I would ask God for communication about something that was going on in my life and I would hold the intention to receive the answer in the form of a sign at some point throughout the day. If I didn't consciously receive the answer before climbing into bed that evening, I would ask the same question the following morning. At first, it took me three or four days to receive the answer. Over time, it became easier and easier to notice the signs. Eventually, I was recognizing the signs on a daily basis and was truly enjoying the process.

After several months of receiving signs on a regular basis, the Holy Spirit suggested that I practice hearing His Voice through conversation with other people. So I began to hold the intention that whoever I spoke with throughout the day would share God's Words with me. I practiced this exercise for several months. It was tricky at first, but as I continued to practice, I began to hear God's Voice through all kinds of people, even my boss! Sometimes, the words were literal. Other times, I would hear God's Messages to me as if they were superimposed over the Words that were actually being said.

Eventually, I came to see that it was all about perception, and as time went on, I started feeling very fulfilled in my communication with God. I may not have been hearing a distinct and audible voice within me, but I was hearing God's Voice nonetheless ... and it felt good.

One spring morning in March of 2000, Candace was about to head off for a two-week retreat to do "The School for The Work" with Byron Katie. While we were lying in bed that morning, we read from *A Course in Miracles*. The lesson of the day was, "God's Voice speaks to me all through the day." As Candace read the lesson out loud, I got really pissed off. I interpreted the lesson to mean hearing a specific audible Voice within me. I was so tired of getting my hopes up and not having it happen that I just started fuming. I could barely contain my anger. My body was literally shaking with rage. I was not going to be let down again!

Candace wasn't aware of what was going on for me, so she finished reading the lesson, closed her eyes, and began to check in with the Holy Spirit. As she shared God's Words coming through her, my anger began to dissipate. At one point, a huge wave of peace came over me, and as it did, the Holy Spirit said something through Candace that It had never said before.... It told me to open my mouth and allow God's Voice to come through me.

Although I was scared, I opened my mouth and started to speak. To my surprise, out came the Voice of my true Self—the Voice for God within me! I don't remember how long I spoke or even what I said, but it was one of the happiest moments of my life. Tears fell from Candace's eyes as the Words came through me. It was truly a heavenly moment.

What makes this day even more special for us is the fact that our daughter, Hannah, was conceived that very morning.... I've been hearing this Voice for Love within me ever since.

✧ EXERCISES – 11 WAYS TO HEAR YOUR INNER VOICE

Everything can be used as a tool or means to hear God. You give everything the meaning that it has, so you can allow anything and everything to serve as your communication with God. It is all a matter of perspective.

There are people who train themselves that when the phone rings, they think, "Oh, that's God calling." They pick it up and they experience God on the other end. Regardless of the situation, what it's about, or whoever may be calling, they experience that God is on the other end and take from that communication whatever message God has for them.

You can allow everything to serve you in hearing God's Voice and allow everything you see, hear, and do to be of God, strictly from how you approach it within your mind. You can use anything as a means to hear God, and for some, it can be helpful to use a consistent method.

There are countless ways to hear God's Voice. In the course of uncovering this Voice within ourselves, we have used a wide variety of methods to strengthen our openness and ability to hear God's Voice with clarity and certainty. Some of these methods are listed below along with step-by-step instructions on how to do them. These exercises are not intended to be exhaustive by any means, but they may provide a starting point for strengthening your faith, openness, and ability to hear God's Voice in whatever way that happens for you. While the exercises are specific, feel free to adapt them to meet your style, personality, or needs in any given moment.

ONE FINAL NOTE BEFORE YOU BEGIN: If you think the exercises in this chapter are too simple to be effective, that is the ego talking. Hearing God's Voice does not need to be a complicated matter, though the ego would say that it does. If you have the desire, *you will hear It.*

So *DO the exercises.*

It is in *doing* them that you will give yourself the *experience* you are seeking. Hearing God's Voice is not an intellectual pursuit. Information and theory are meaningful only in their ability to inspire you to *take action*; they cannot create the experience for you. If you really want to hear God's Voice within you in a clear and recognizable way, *DO* the exercises and see what happens. Remember, anything and everything can be used as a means to hear God's Voice.

SILENCE

Being in silence does not mean that no communication is occurring—it is quite the contrary. When one has quieted the mind and is being present in the silence of their Right-Mind, in the silence of Pure Being, the Light and Love and Truth that *is* this Presence can fill the mind with understanding, wisdom, and a sense of knowingness that is truly freeing and filled with peace and faith.

You may not consciously perceive the communication that is unfolding within you and being transmitted to you, and yet communication *is* happening. It is for this reason that one can sit in silence for long periods of time, or only for a moment, and when they open their eyes, their entire reality has changed. Their problems have fallen away and they are certain about what step to take or how to perceive. In that moment, they are being the presence of Love.

Know that sitting in silence is indeed a wonderful way to hear God's Voice, and it has the potential to serve you in all the ways you desire.

STEPS

1. Sit alone in a quiet place where there are no distractions.
2. Close your eyes and allow your mind to quiet, using whatever technique or form of meditation you desire.
3. When your thoughts have quieted, allow yourself to bask in the Love of God and God's Voice. Feel It. Breath It in. Enjoy It.
4. When thoughts arise, extend Love to them and allow your mind to return to experiencing the Presence of Love that you are.
5. Allow the mind to go deeper and deeper in this experience, and allow the peace and love to grow stronger and stronger.
6. When you are ready, open your eyes.
7. Notice in what ways you feel differently from when you started. Is there a situation or thing in your life that you now see differently? What shift in perception has taken place within you?

BOOKS

Reading a book that is filled with Truth can give you more of a sense of Who and What God really is and this can lead to a deeper sense of connectedness and communion with God. There is also the experience of taking a book off the shelf and opening it to any page with the intention that whatever message, direction, or insight God has for you will be there on that page. It may mean something different to someone else, but as you read it, you will glean your own message from it.

STEPS

1. Determine what you want to know, understand, or

receive and then share that with God in whatever way you wish.

2. Pray or hold the intention that you are being guided to the right book, the right page, and the right paragraph to receive the answer that is in your highest good.

3. You may already have a book in mind or not. If you do not and you are selecting a book from a bookshelf, allow yourself to reach for a book naturally, having faith that whatever book you select is perfect.

4. Open the book and point to a paragraph.

5. Read what you have pointed to and allow the words or the message to sink in. It may or may not be obvious. If you do not understand, continue to seek its meaning. As you hold the intention to hear the Truth that it has for you, you will open up to hearing the message that God has given you.

Spiritual Cards, Runes, and Other Symbols

One can use various types of spiritual cards, runes, or other symbols with intention so that when you hold a thought, say a prayer, seek an answer, or seek guidance or connection, you will be able to receive communication from God as you turn over a card or pick up a stone, and with that intention, you can trust the communication.

Steps

1. Determine what you want to know, understand, or receive and then share that with God in whatever way you wish.

2. Pray or hold the intention that you are being guided

to the card, stone, or symbol that is in your highest good.

3. Select and turn over the card or stone without analyzing or second-guessing your natural impulse.

4. Read the message(s) provided in the book that came with the cards or runes or be aware of any thoughts or insights that come to your mind. If you do not understand the answer that comes to you, continue to seek its meaning. As you hold the intention to hear the Truth that it has for you, you will open up to receive the message that God has given you.

SIGNS

You may have a particular situation going on that is very troubling or confusing, and you are in need of clear direction. As you go through your day, you can ask for signs. When you have the intention that God will give you signs and show you the way, you will be able to see the signs. They are always there, though without the intention to see them, you miss them. You have gotten to this point using signs, whether they have been consciously witnessed or not.

You can determine for yourself that whatever messages and directions you need will be given to you. Then as you go through your day, you might literally see a sign with guidance on it. You might open a newspaper and see what it is that you need to do. You may get a phone call, encounter a person, experience a situation, or witness something that you realize is the answer for you. It is powerful to do this in troubling times and yet you can go through your whole life every day asking for signs, receiving signs, and allowing their messages to be made clear to you so that you move continually in the direction of Truth. When you are very clear about what you desire, you will be given all that you need to get there.

STEPS

1. Become clear about what you are seeking and then ask God to show you a sign as His reply to your request or question.
2. Allow yourself to be completely open as to what the sign may look like and how it may be given.
3. Pray or hold the intention that you will recognize the sign as it is given.
4. Be mindful and aware throughout your day or week of what you see, think, hear, or experience and know God's communication to you may take any form.
5. Be patient and have faith that you and God are working together to create a sign that you *will* receive.

DREAMS

Just as you imagine that you are living a life in the world in a body, that your body tires and you rest, you sleep and you dream, that is what is representative of your "real life," you are in a very long sleep with long vivid dreams. Just as you glean messages from the lives you appear to live and the experiences you appear to have in the world, you are really just having a dream. And when you have a dream within the dream—when you are in a body and you rest and you sleep and you have a dream—you can glean messages from these dreams as well.

You may wake up in the night or in the morning with a dream on your mind and you might ask within you for insight or direction as to what that dream means and allow yourself to receive whatever answer or message you are given. When one doesn't ask, the answer doesn't come. So by asking, your answer will come. It is only a matter of when. Allow your dreams to serve you if you desire, just as what appears to be your life now is serving you.

STEPS

1. Ask God to help you understand what message your dream has for you and then listen for His reply.
2. Be aware of any thoughts, feelings, or insights that come to you and trust what you receive.
3. If you do not experience receiving the answer right away, allow yourself to receive the answer later in the day or in the week.
4. Be open to receiving the answer in any form, such as a sign, an insight, or through something you read or hear.

Note: You can also seek guidance and direction before going to bed and hold the intention to receive the answer while you sleep or in your dreams.

LISTENING TO OTHERS

In remembering that God's Voice speaks through all of God's Children, you can allow yourself to trust and have faith that God can speak to you through another. So you have stated your prayer, intention, and desire for Truth, and then someone in front of you in the grocery line turns around and makes a statement to you or another person in line and it is exactly what you need to hear. You can do this for direct guidance, for remembrance, for an answer, or for whatever you need. Just hold the intention that whoever stands near you will share God's Words with you and you will be able to pick out the

If you desire to hear God, all around you is God speaking, but if you do not like the delivery or you do not value the delivery, God's Voice won't be received. If you are open and willing to allow God's Voice to take any form through your trust and your faith, by desiring to hear God, you will.

message as it is being delivered.

It may be that you are out in the world and you hear a child say, "Let's play!" and those words ring true for you. There is something about that tiny communication and you think, "Oh, I need to play. I need to have more play in my life," and you bring yourself to a park, play a game, or do something more playfully rather than seriously in your life. You approach things with a more playful attitude.

It can be the simplest, most mundane, everyday type of communication, but with the intention that you will hear God in what another speaks, you will hear a message and there will be a certain feeling or experience within you that you know this message was meant for you. It rings true for you and you can apply it in your life in ways that truly serve you.

Steps

1. Pray or hold the intention that whoever you are with is sharing God's Words with you.
2. Each time you hear someone speak, remind yourself that you are listening to God's Voice.
3. Ask yourself, "What is God saying to me through this person?" The message may be literal, symbolic, or implied. It may come through the person's words, emotion, tone, or intention. It does not matter. If the answer or message is not apparent, ask again, "What is God saying to me through this person?
4. Trust the thoughts, insights, and messages that come to you. God is speaking to you nonstop, through everything, if you are willing to listen.

SHARING GOD'S VOICE WITH OTHERS

You can also have the intention of being a messenger to another. You can have the intention that you are able to say whatever another needs to hear. You can ask that it come through you in your communication with another, and you can state that intention each day or before certain encounters so that you will know that whatever it is you are saying is the appropriate thing for that situation and you can trust that it is right.

The goal is not to have the person hear God, because that is their business, their choice, their path, and their free will. Your intention is that you speak messages of Truth, and that is different. What they do with that, if anything, is up to them. For you, you gain the validation or acknowledgment for having had the thought to do that, the intention to follow through, and the willingness to allow the message of Truth to come through you, and that's the end of it. Enjoy it for the experience that it is rather than what someone else may gain from it.

STEPS

1. Say a prayer or hold the intention that you can and will speak God's Words in a given situation or throughout your day, to a specific person, or to anyone around you.
2. Continue to hold this intention as you speak.
3. Knowing that God speaks to people wherever they are and in whatever ways they are able to receive, allow your words to flow freely. Trust what you say and how you say it.
4. When you are finished speaking, thank God for the opportunity to share His Words and give thanks to yourself for being willing to share them.

Everything can be used as a tool or means to hear God. You give everything the meaning that it has, so you can allow anything and everything to serve as your communication with God. It is all a matter of perspective.

HEARING THIS VOICE IN THE WORLD

It seems that hearing God's Voice within is a difficult thing or a special gift; however, hearing this Voice within is the most natural experience one can have. Hearing God's Voice in the world is where it becomes more difficult because what one hears in the world isn't automatically experienced as loving and kind. When one allows themselves to hear with the ears of the Holy Spirit, everything can be communication from God and can be experienced as loving and kind. This is the path toward overcoming the world—seeing the Truth of it; experiencing God and God's Voice within it. This is how one overcomes the world, not by leaving it, or destroying it, but by seeing the Truth in it.

Spend an hour focused on hearing God's Voice in the world. Go to the park, or a store, or anywhere with lots of people, and sit for an entire hour and listen as if you are wearing the ears of the Holy Spirit. Listen to every communication with Love—with your Right-Mind. Whatever comes, ask the Holy Spirit, "How can I hear this the way you would? What is really being said? How can I hear the Truth in the communications that I'm hearing?"

The Truth is—only love is being spoken—but one does not always hear it that way. As you sit for that hour listening, asking, and seeking, you are training yourself to hear with ears of Love. You are training yourself to go past judgments, worldly thoughts and fears, and to hear only the Truth of the communication. It would be valuable to do this on an ongoing basis. Determine for yourself how much time you can commit to doing this. Put it on your calendar, and really use that time to train yourself to hear as the Holy Spirit would.

STEPS

1. Set a date, time, and location to practice this exercise for one hour.
2. Take yourself to that location on that date and time and just start listening.
3. No matter what you hear or how it sounds, ask the Holy Spirit to help you "hear" that communication, sound, or whatever it may be, as loving.
4. Continue to do this over and over again with everything you hear.
5. When the hour is done, thank God for helping you hear His Voice in all things.
6. Notice how your understanding and experience of hearing this Voice has changed as a result.

JOURNALING

For many people, the opportunity to sit with themselves, God, a notebook, and a pen is something that is very intimate and rewarding. One can sit with a pen and paper and have the intention that God communicate with them, to them, or through them, and then begin to write down the thoughts they have while they are intending to be connected with God. It doesn't necessarily mean that a big booming Voice speaks in their head and tells them all of the secrets of the universe. It means that you may have certain thoughts come to mind. You may have insights, perspectives, or situations come up and you can make note of those and put them into a journal.

Regardless of whether you understand or receive great value from these thoughts in the moment, you can later sit with this journal and look at what is written there. If you do this on an ongoing basis, you will begin to see themes and messages that carry over repeatedly. These are things you would want to take notice of.

A situation may continue to come to mind, and as you make note of it, you might become aware that it is something that is unresolved and needs to be completed. You may notice that there are some things you need to do something about. You might become aware that these things are either distractions away from God or things that will take you closer in your communion with God. Writing these things down can help you have a sense of these within your mind. It is an exercise in being aware of your thoughts, and as you continue to intend to be in communion with God and hear God, you can use the thoughts that come up to help you deepen your relationship with God.

You may have thoughts that this isn't real or possible, such as "I can't communicate with God." Make note of that and ask yourself, "Is it true? Is it true that I can't communicate with God in this way?" Absolutely not. Give yourself the freedom of recognizing that those thoughts are just universal thoughts that the ego promotes. There are many people who believe that it is not possible to communicate with God, and that doesn't have to be your truth. In your reality, it is possible. Therefore, you will be able to do it.

As you become aware of what goes on in your mind, you can work with your thinking. You may notice that you need to shift or change your perspective so you can see things differently. You can gain messages of Truth that carry you through the day or bring peace to a situation. You can become aware of how to handle something or know that something needs to be taken care of. This then becomes prayer and meditation with God that you are simply taking notes on.

STEPS

1. Sit alone in a quiet place where there are no distractions.
2. Close your eyes and allow your mind to quiet using

whatever process or form of meditation you desire.

3. When your thoughts have quieted and you experience a connection with your Right-Mind, say a prayer or hold the intention that God will communicate with you, to you, and through you when you begin writing.

4. Open your eyes and begin to write down any thoughts that come to you. Don't worry if they are only single words, repeating words, or sentence fragments. You may acknowledge a particular thought or you may just have an impulse to write something down. Allow yourself to write freely without judgment or analysis. Continue to hold the intention of being in your Right-Mind and having God's Voice be expressed through your writing.

5. When you are finished, thank God for working with you to hear and manifest His Voice through your writing.

6. Periodically review your journal for themes and messages.

HEARING THIS VOICE WITHIN YOU

When one prays, they are communicating with God. They are the one doing the talking. When one meditates, they are listening to God and God is the One doing the talking. One of the most beneficial tool for having an ongoing communication with God comes from meditation, which can include prayer.

If you are able to maintain your focus, attention, and intention on God, it is difficult for other things to distract you away. When you have your mind stayed on God and you continue to reconnect with that thought and that intention over and over again, when you are just there to join with,

It is so easy to perceive God in the one in front of you when you can perceive God in yourself. When God is all you see in you, God will be all you see in your brother; it would not be possible to see anything else.

experience, and hear God, or when you are willing and able to listen to whatever it is God has to say to you or share with you, there is no room in the mind for anything else. It becomes a very focused moment with God.

You may say a prayer. You may say a mantra with intention. You can invite God to join you and ask God to be with you, or you can sit and wait for God's Words to come to you. You might ask questions and wait for answers. You may talk to God as if you were telling a dear friend how much you appreciate them in your life and all that they have done for you and given you. You may experience your gratitude for God's Presence and just wallow in thankfulness. You may ask the Holy Spirit or Jesus to communicate with you.

You will be receiving Truth in all of those forms, in whatever way you can hear God's Message. Continue to invite It. Continue to seek It. Continue to receive It, and know that you are having that connection regardless of what your conscious experience might be. You may hear words. You may see images. You may think certain thoughts that are incredibly loving, inspiring, and filled with Truth. You may have a physical experience. The more that you engage in this, the more you will recognize how it is that *you* hear God. You will become clearer about what it is you are receiving and in what ways, and you will begin to understand the best ways for you to hear God. What are the most powerful, impacting, meaningful, or simplest ways for *you*?

Perhaps you might begin with starting or ending your day with God, and then eventually both. Having more time devoted to this practice will help you become familiar with the process and comfortable with the connection, and eventually you will hear and understand more. You will receive guidance and direction throughout the day that will be more obvious to you, and you will have more overall peace, faith, and trust in your life. Eventually there will be less seeking of guidance and direction because you will just know and understand that everything is perfect. Eventually, this communion begins to stretch between the mornings and the evenings and the times during the day and it begins to fill in the gaps between those set-aside times, so that more and more you are having this communion within your mind, this experience of God ... the words, the feelings, the guidance, direction, and love. As you take that into more moments of your day, it will one day fill in all of the gaps so that all you have is communication and communion with God and that will become your reality.

DavidPaul: What is the advantage of hearing words from God versus experiencing God in countless other ways?

If it isn't broken, don't fix it. If one is experiencing God and has a full, complete, and rewarding relationship with God, and they aren't seeking more, this book is not for them. It is for people who would like to hear God and think they don't. These might even be people who have had experiences with God, have felt God, have known God, and yet they can't maintain it or attain it whenever they want. They are striving toward that relationship.

For many in a humanly form, it is difficult to project onto God that God can be anything other than some type of grand humanly form. The way that humans communicate is with words, primarily. Of course there are actions, deeds, expressions, and looks, though the most abundant type of communication between human forms is talking. Humans love to talk. Therefore, it is imagined that God is a talker also. When you have this concept of God, and it is difficult to have a different one being in a human form yourself, you therefore seek the type of communication you're comfortable and familiar with. It is not that there is an advantage to one over the other, only that if your relationship with God is not everything you want it to be, then the Reality that every single person has God's Voice within them and can access that Voice if they want to is a wonderful reminder and gift. This book is not suggesting that everyone should do this, only that everyone *could* if they so desire.

STEPS

1. Sit alone in a quiet place where there are no distractions.

2. Close your eyes and allow your mind to quiet using whatever process or form of meditation you desire.

3. When your thoughts have quieted and you experience a connection with your Right-Mind, begin a conversation with God, either in your mind or out loud, whichever you prefer. Share with God your intentions, fears, hopes, dreams, or anything else you want to share.

4. When you are done communicating what is in your heart, ask God to speak to you, then sit quietly and listen for God's Voice. God *will* communicate back to you. If a loving thought comes to you or you think of a loving word or phrase, you are hearing God's Voice. Allow yourself to receive those thoughts and words, and allow them to continue. You are hearing God's Voice within you!

5. If after a few minutes you do not hear or sense anything, imagine moving the radio tuner within your mind to God's Station, to the frequency of God's Voice within you.

6. Be open to however God's Voice may sound. It might be a faint thought or idea. It might sound like a whisper, or It might sound like a wise version of your own inner voice. It may not "sound" like anything. You may feel something, sense something, or see a

picture or color in your mind. Allow all of it to be a communication from God. If you notice something and do not understand its meaning, ask God for understanding and then listen again.

7. If you are still unaware of hearing God's Voice, you might allow God's Voice to speak through you. Open your mouth with this intention and allow yourself to speak God's Words. Allow whatever comes through to come through, no matter what it sounds like ... repeating words, broken sentences, the same sentences over and over, or the most beautiful words you have ever heard. It doesn't matter. When you give God a voice, you give yourself the opportunity to receive God's Voice.

8. For some people, it is difficult to *sit* and hear God's Voice. You may need to get up and walk with a certain intention or mindfulness. As you walk, go through the process of inviting God to join with you and then allow yourself to hear God's Voice. Keep your mind on God so that whatever happens around you is irrelevant. Allow the Words to come to you and through you.

How Do I Know Which Voice I am Hearing?

DavidPaul: In the process of gaining our certainty about hearing God's Voice in the world, there have been times when Candace and I have questioned whether we were hearing God's Voice or hearing the ego. How can one truly know which voice they are hearing?

There are, often times, many voices running around in one's head and more often than not, these are the voices of criticism, judgment, attack, or blame. They tell you what you did wrong, what you should have done differently, or how you could have done better. They tell you what that person did wrong, what they should not have done, and how they should have done it better. Those types of communications are the voice of the ego.

You know you are hearing God's Voice when what you hear is filled with Truth. It may not always be what you want to hear, so you may think, "This Voice is telling me that this person in front of me who I have fallen in love with is not the person I will spend my life with." You might feel angry at that Voice and you might think it is the ego because you do not like the answer, and yet, if you ask this Voice within, "Is this person in front of me the one I will spend my life with?" and if you hear an answer filled with Truth, whether it answers your question or not, whether you like the answer or not, and there is no attack or blame or criticism or judgment, you can know you are hearing the Voice for God. Once you enter into judgment, attack, and blame, you can know you are no longer hearing God's Voice.

In particular, how you know you are hearing God's Voice is because you have asked to hear God's Voice. You have asked God to join with you, communicate with you, and give you guidance, direction, or Truth. On one level or another, you have asked for that Voice. The ego, on the other hand, just rambles on and on within the mind without invitation because once you made the ego, the invitation was open. You cannot now un-invite the ego, but you *can* quiet the ego.

When you notice that what you are hearing in your mind is not of Truth or of Love, you can stop for a moment and inquire within yourself as to what you are hearing, and if it is something that is judgmental or attacking, you can acknowledge that. If you want to, you can thank the ego for that input and then make a decision within yourself to hear Truth instead. You make the decision to no longer participate in that which is not real and you say, "God, I would like to hear Truth."

It is similar to changing the radio station on your stereo. When a song comes on that you do not like, you click a button or turn the dial and you move on to the next song. You can do the same in your mind when you hear communication that you don't like, that is not serving you, or feels painful. You can say instead, "I want to hear God's Station," and you click over to that one and ask God to communicate with you. Words may come into your mind or it may be a feeling or a sense that God or God's Voice is with you. Regardless of what form your connection or communication takes, by turning the dial to God's Station, you quiet the ego and turn up the volume on the Voice for Love and Truth within you.

The challenge then is to notice when you are *not* listening to the Holy Spirit. Ultimately, there are only two voices to listen to—the ego or God's Voice. If the one you are listening to is painful, then you would want to choose differently. It has simply become a habit to take in, absorb, think about, and act upon all that comes into your mind from the ego.

When you notice that your thinking is painful, which could be anything from, "This water is probably contaminated," when you pour yourself a glass of water, to "I am late. I never have enough time. I can't get everything done," to "I wonder why my father hasn't called. He should have called by now. Maybe he doesn't want to talk to me," you give yourself the opportunity to choose differently. You give yourself the choice to think with your Right-Mind instead, so that you can have peace and faith in those moments, rather than pain. It is those simple, seemingly benign thoughts that you encounter millions of times each day that are the thoughts that cause you pain without even realizing it.

It is the choosing that is the most difficult. Hearing God is your most natural ability. It is your natural right and gift and

If you want to hear God's Voice in the world, give God's Voice a mouth and vocal cords to speak with. Give your Self a pen to write with. Join with this part of your Self that is the Holy Spirit, that is the Voice for Love, and express your Self using the body as a communication device. BE the Holy Spirit in form to hear the Holy Spirit in form.

that which has never been gone from you except with your thinking. But choosing to hear that Voice, choosing to quiet the ego and turn up the volume on God, can be challenging indeed. In order to do that, you must become aware of your thoughts, how they are serving you or not serving you, and replace the ones that are not serving you with thoughts of Truth and Peace.

When you have thoughts that are serving you, acknowledge them, give thanks for them, take a moment to appreciate them, and continue to seek more. The more that you practice changing stations, the easier it will be to stay tuned to the frequency that truly serves you. Ultimately, there will come a day when your radio tuner is programmed only to the station of your true Voice and it does not leave that station any more. Eventually all you will hear is God's Voice, Right-Thinking, Truth, and Reality in any given situation, which would then mean you have been restored to your natural state.

One thinks that this goal is monumental, impossible, daunting, and yet all it means is that you are being restored to your natural state, that of only hearing the Voice of your Creator, only hearing Truth, and only seeing Truth as a result. You no longer hear or see the world through the eyes and ears of the ego, as was Jesus's experience. The peace, comfort, and love that come from only hearing this Voice, no matter what seems to be happening in the world, is invaluable because Love, Peace, and Truth is all there is. There is no opposite. There is no up and down, back and forth, left and right. There is only Love, Peace, and Truth. There is nothing to compare it to or contrast it with, but only to rejoice in that restored state.

When Jesus appeared to walk upon the earth, his goal was to only hear God's Voice. His goal was to no longer hear the ego or participate in any of the ideas of the ego but rather hear Truth, follow Truth, and share Truth. Over the course of that lifetime, Jesus accomplished that goal and only heard Truth. Being in a body and having experienced the ego, Jesus was able to understand the thoughts in the minds of the ones in front of him, while at the same time knowing that none of the thoughts of the world were true.

When one came to him and talked about their life, their situation in the world, sickness, death, and so on, Jesus heard them and knew from where they were speaking and yet did not believe in what they were saying and did not join them in those thoughts. He had so much certainty that what they were saying was not true, whether they were sick or maimed or dying, because he could only hear Truth. He could touch them and talk to them with so much clarity and so much confidence and Truth that their illness, injury, or dying would fall away because in fact it was not true. It was not that he was a miracle worker so much as that he did not believe the illusions of the world and could not participate in them. He could not see illness or injury. He could not see dying or death as it is known in the world, and when one saw through his eyes, it all fell away.

It seems to those in the world that the task of hearing only God's Voice is so enormous and daunting that it could not be possible, and yet that is the whole purpose of Jesus's life—to show you that it is possible. Jesus was not special in the sense of being more capable or being more loved by God to be able to hear only the Holy Spirit. Jesus just dedicated every moment of his life on the earth to that end and, of course, it came about. That is the only difference. Different goals, different dreams, different desires, and different outcomes. You are not different from Jesus in your ability to pursue the same goal or in your ability to carry out the same dream and the same intention.

Jesus fabricated a most horrific death by the world's standards to show that even while the worst was happening, it did not matter. It was not real. Jesus did not perceive that death. Jesus only perceived that which was Real. Jesus only perceived God's Son, God, and the Holy Spirit, which has absolutely nothing to do with the world, anything in the world, bodies, death, or crucifixions. Jesus loved equally the ones who seemed to appear in front of him, be they his mother or brother or persecutors because he understood that they were Him—they were God's Son.

When one can hear only God's Voice, they can perceive only that Voice in the one in front of them. Because God's Voice is in everyone, it is easy to perceive Truth in the one in front of you. It is so easy to perceive God in the one in front of you when you can perceive God in yourself. When God is all you see in you, God will be all you see in your brother; it would not be possible to see anything else.

Becoming very clear about what it is you truly want and then dedicating every moment to that with nothing else but your thinking, you too can have that which you seek. One thinks that to dedicate every moment to their purpose means being on their knees in a monastery somewhere or to be of service like Mother Teresa. What it means is that in every moment you are aware of what you are thinking and you choose the kind of thinking that serves you and the world so that only that which you truly desire can unfold. Know that God's Voice is with you every thought of the way, is there for the choosing, and has as Its only desire, to serve you.

✧ EXERCISE – BEING MINDFUL

Set aside a quiet time, turn off the phone, put a note on the door, get comfortable, and close your eyes. You can pray. You can meditate. Spend as many minutes as you would like doing either or both. Connect with God. Connect with yourself. Feel

God's Voice within you. Make the statement to yourself that you would like to hear God's Voice, and imagine that as you make that declaration, the Holy Spirit accepts your invitation and joins with you. It has no other function but to do so.

You can either begin a dialogue with God and listen for the answer, or you can sit and notice the thoughts that come into your mind. The thoughts that are loving, kind, and truthful come from your Right-Mind, from God's Voice within you, while the ones that are not are the thoughts of the ego. As you notice the thoughts of the ego, do not worry about, be frightened by, or be angry with them. Just note, "Right now, I am thinking with the ego mind," and put your attention back on God-Mind and allow your thoughts again to come from God-Mind. Allow yourself to engage in this practice of noticing the thoughts, allowing yourself to recognize where they come from, not judging them or fearing them, just noticing them, and continue to refocus on the thoughts of the Holy Spirit.

You may become distracted at some point and go on some adventure somewhere in your thinking; when you notice this, just bring yourself back. There is nothing to be disappointed in or mad at. Just bring yourself back to here and now, with the thought, desire, and intention to connect with Right-Mindedness. Interact with your thoughts in this way for as long as you can, and when you are complete, you can give thanks to God for the Right-Mindedness that you have available to you at all times. It is there for your choosing and only to serve you, and nothing you can think or do could ever change that.

What Does This Voice Sound Like to Us?

Candace: When I first heard the Holy Spirit, it was an unexpected surprise. It was as if a flood gate had opened in my mind and waves of communication came rushing in. It reminded me of what it might be like to lose your voice for a long time and finally get it back. There was enthusiasm and passion in the words I heard and almost an urgency in their delivery. The words were so loving and beautiful and comforting, and they felt so good to hear.

I talked with this Voice throughout the entire first day, and for several days thereafter, asking questions and learning more about Who and What It was. I didn't know much about the Holy Spirit at the time so it was all new to me. When I would drift off into other thoughts, I would hear the Voice calling me to come back. I would immediately tune back into the Voice and reconnect with this ongoing conversation.

I remember interviewing for a job as a hospice counselor during those first few days. Because I was so connected with this Voice, I was able to hear It over whatever else was going on. I took this Voice into the interview and used It to answer questions about how I would handle a variety of situations involving death and dying. With the help of God's Voice, I answered these questions to the surprise and disbelief of the interviewers. My responses were so filled with Truth and deep acceptance and peace around the topic that the interviewers said they could not hire me because I was too comfortable with death, and in thinking that death was not possible, I would not be a good counselor. Of course from their perspective, this was true. I, on the other hand, thought I would have been a great counselor.

Shortly thereafter, the Voice began to fade and the sounds of the world began to get louder and louder. It was around this time that DavidPaul sent someone to me to receive communication from the Holy Spirit. This began my process of hearing God's Voice for others and soon became the usual way I heard this Voice for myself.

When I first began to hear God's Words "on demand," through sharing specific messages with others at a specific time rather than hearing them spontaneously within myself, it was a big leap of faith for me. I'm not sure now why I thought I could do this, but it just unfolded that way. At first I would hear, "You are loved and you are whole." This became almost like a password between me and the Holy Spirit so that I would know I was connected. Over time, the password became unnecessary and the sessions would begin with, "Greetings and blessings to you, precious one(s)." This greeting continues to this day and is always comforting and reassuring to hear.

The first dozen or so times that I shared God's Voice with others, I would literally read the words on a screen in my mind. It was as if the words were being slowly typed, and I would read them out loud. There was no time delay between seeing the words and speaking them so I wasn't able to think before I spoke. As an individual session with someone went on, the words would come faster and I would begin to grasp what the message was really about.

With each subsequent session, the words came faster and faster, until one day they stopped appearing in front of me and I just heard them. At first, I would hear a line and then convey that line, hear another line and then convey that line. Eventually, the words came through with no delay between hearing them and speaking them, and the style became much more conversational. Sometimes the Voice would joke with people and tease them playfully in ways I never would have imagined.

When the words began to flow freely with others, I started to see a movie in my head of what was being said. Sometimes I would see a picture, but mostly I would see a movie playing and that would tell me more about what was going on than the words themselves. Sometimes the movie would allow me to see the bigger picture of what was being said. Other times, it showed me details that weren't mentioned and I would sometimes have a different sense of the message.

The sessions I did with others were primarily about teaching them how to hear this Voice for themselves. The Holy Spirit told me early on that my agreement with It was to help others learn how to hear God's Voice. I didn't sign up to be a go between, but rather to inspire others and demonstrate this Gift we all have from God. When I asked, "Why me?" the Holy Spirit told me that I was a good example for people because anyone who knew me would say, "If she can do it, anybody can!"

When I hear this Voice now, It is not something I hear in my head, as much as a Voice that comes out when I open my mouth to share It. When I do hear the Holy Spirit in my head, It sounds like an old friend talking to me. I have to concentrate deeply to stay tuned in to the Voice and the words flow into me as if I'm sitting with a trusted partner. To this day, I sometimes doubt whether something will come through me when I open my mouth or worry that what I say won't make sense. But I keep opening my mouth with the faith I have gained from many years of practice, trusting that whatever happens will be perfect.

DavidPaul: When I first heard God's Voice within me that morning with Candace, It didn't sound like I thought it would. For years, I imagined it would be like talking on the phone or hearing a loud Voice within me, but when it actually happened, there was no separate or distinct voice. I was hearing the words for the first time as I was speaking them out loud. At first, I didn't think it was really happening, that maybe I was somehow making it up, but when I heard the words coming out of my mouth, I could feel the Holy Spirit within them, and I knew they were not mine.

This is the closest description I can think of to share what it is like to hear this Voice within me: Imagine standing in front of a group of your closest friends. One of them suddenly says, "Tell us a story about a grasshopper and a bumblebee." And before you have a chance to think, someone else yells, "Go!" and you have to start speaking immediately without knowing how it's going to start, what's going to be said next, or where the story is going to go. You just have to open your mouth and start speaking ... so you do. Within moments, the story begins to take on a life of its own, and you too begin to listen to the story coming out of your mouth. Surprisingly, it's interesting, intriguing, and enjoyable to listen to, and before you know it, you're just as excited as everyone else to see where the story will end. Finally, the story ends and your friends give you a standing ovation. It was a brilliant story, and you agree. You don't know how you pulled it off, but you did, and you're grateful for it.

When I first started hearing this Voice, I heard It only during meditation, while my eyes were closed. As my confidence grew, I began to experiment. First, I practiced doing it with my eyes open. Then I started doing it as I walked through the park near our house. While I walked, I would feel this Loving Presence within and around me, and when I was ready, I would ask this Voice to speak to me. I would then open my mouth and start speaking. When people walked by, I would pause, smile, and then start speaking again after they passed. This quickly became my favorite way of hearing God's Voice because the words seemed to come easily and naturally when I walked.

Over time, I began to experiment with saying the words silently to myself instead of saying them out loud, as if I were reading a book or silently talking to myself. I first started doing this in the morning while lying in bed, not wanting to wake up Candace by talking out loud. I then started doing it around other people, like at the gym or in other public places. At first, I was easily distracted by everyone around me, but the more I practiced, the easier it became.

To this day, whether I'm speaking the words out loud or silently to myself, I still have to physically form the words in some way. Even if I'm not speaking the words out loud, I can still feel my throat and tongue moving as I silently say the words. I've always wanted to hear this Voice without having to form the words myself, but I've never experienced that.

One day, I was feeling frustrated about the way I heard this Voice within me and wanted to understand why I couldn't hear a more distinctive Voice within me, so I decided to ask for some insight. This is what I heard:

Greetings and blessings to you, precious one. Indeed it is a joyous occasion to gather together with you in this way. There are no specific ways that God seeks to speak to His children. He has no goals or preferences for how He speaks. He speaks however His children are best able to hear Him. He speaks to them in ways they are able to receive and in ways that serve them in their growth and in their awareness of their Union with Him.

You are one who seeks to know your Oneness with God this lifetime. To perceive a separation between His Voice and yours would not support this goal in the way you might think. To always experience His Voice, His Words, and His Thoughts to be separate from your own, to be different in such a way that you can point to them and find them and experience them as different from your own voice does not serve you.

There are many who would benefit from this way of hearing God's Voice. There are many who would use this way of hearing to further their awareness of their Oneness with God. Eventually, their experience of Oneness would evolve, and as it did, so would their experience of hearing. Relationship is not a static experience. Your relationship with God, yourself, and the world is constantly changing, as is your communication. Even if you were to hear God's Voice as separate, over time, your communication with God would evolve and grow and change.

You hear and experience God's Voice within you as your Highest Self, the part of your mind that is always connected to God-Mind, the part of your mind that you feel and know to be You, which is also connected with Truth and with God. It is there where God communicates with you, and it is there within yourself that God's Voice is heard. This is always the case, and yet it can be perceived differently by different people. There are many who do not yet experience that aspect of their Self, do not yet know that part of their Self, and are not yet connected and aware of that aspect of their Mind. For them, they experience these words and these thoughts to be separate, and yet they can never be separate.

You were already connected and feeling this part of yourself and knowing this part of yourself when you started hearing God's Voice. It is because of this that you did not experience this Voice as separate from your own, as separate from your mind. As each person awakens to this Voice, he or she will experience It differently, hear It differently, and relate to It in their own unique way. Know that you hear God's Voice in just the right way for you, just as another hears it in just the right way for them.

Blessings to you precious one. Amen.

DavidPaul: To this day, my hearing of God's Voice continues to evolve and strengthen, and I still experiment with where, when, and how I can more fully access this Presence in my life. Although it has only been a few years since I first started hearing God's Voice in this way, I am repeatedly amazed by what I hear and how it has impacted my life. I can only imagine what it will be like with another fifty or so potential years of practice ahead of me....

A Big Booming Voice and the Secret to Hearing

DavidPaul: Many people believe that when they hear God's Voice it's going to sound like a loud, audible Voice within them. We've seen it in the movies. We've read about it in the Bible. We've even heard stories of others who have "heard a voice" within them. The fact is, many people really do hear God's Voice like this. We may have even heard it like this once or twice ourselves, so we natually believe God's Voice is going to sound like this again in the future. Even using the term "hearing" may reinforce this belief within us, though using other words like "perceive" or "experience" have limitations as well. For some, this unconscious belief or expectation of hearing an audible voice within them can be a major barrier to hearing this Voice at all—just as it was for me.

If you do not experience hearing this Presence of Love within you in some way, no matter how patient, persistent, and willing you feel you have been—especially when journaling or listening to this Voice within you—it's important to let go of the concept that some outside entity or presence is going to speak *to you*. In Truth, you *are* this Voice for Love within you. If you want to hear God's Voice in the world, give God's Voice a mouth and vocal cords to speak with. Give your Self a pen to write with. Join with this part of your Self that *is* the Holy Spirit, that *is* the Voice for Love, and express your Self using the body as a communication device. BE the Holy Spirit in form to hear the Holy Spirit in form.

If you hear nothing but silence yet know you are in your Right-Mind—feeling connected, feeling God's Love, and willing to hear—*open your mouth and start speaking, or pick up your pen and start writing*. There is nothing outside of you that is going to express this Voice in the world. *You are It.* Express, speak, and write with your Right-Mind and you will

Y ou can talk about exercise all you want, but until you go to the gym and get on a machine, lift some weights, or start a class, nothing happens. It is the same with hearing this Voice for Love within you. You can talk about it all you want, and yet if you don't sit down and make that connection, it is only a theory.

be hearing, sharing, and *being* God's Voice in the world. For those who try and try, and try and try, and still hear nothing—no matter what they do—being in their Right-Mind and opening their mouth or picking up a pen *is* the secret to hearing. This is how I hear and share God's Voice, and it just may be the key that unlocks the door for you as well.

VALIDATING OURSELVES

DavidPaul: Allowing ourselves to hear and speak God's Voice can be a frightening experience. It's natural to feel incredibly vulnerable, uncertain, or afraid in the moment that we make this commitment and open our mouth. We too have felt this way on many occasions. In these moments, ask God to help you let go of any fear or uncertainty so that you can open your mouth and hear His Voice within you. You may hear only a few words or thoughts, or you may hear the most Truthful and loving communication you have ever heard. Regardless of what you hear, the more you connect with this Voice, the louder It becomes.

A big part of coming to hear this Voice in my life was the result of acknowledging where and how I *was* already hearing this Voice. By learning to validate my ability to hear God's Voice through signs, for example, my beliefs about my inability to "hear" this Voice began to change; and as I practiced and learned how to acknowledge and hear this Voice in other ways, I began to see that I didn't have to hear this Voice in my head to experience and believe that I could hear God. Eventually, these other ways of hearing became so fulfilling that my need to hear God's Voice in a particular way, i.e. as an audible Voice within me, soon disappeared. Even though I wasn't hearing this Voice the way I originally thought I would, all of these other ways of "hearing" God were so rich and rewarding that I knew I really was hearing God's Voice in my life.

It was this conviction and reality that ultimately led to my first experience of hearing this Inner Wisdom as a clear and discernible Voice within me. So as you practice hearing God's Voice in various ways, validate yourself and the successes that you have. As your validation builds, you will create the perception, experience, and belief that you *are* hearing this Voice in your life. Once this perception takes root, hearing God's Voice in other ways will naturally unfold.

HEARING IN A VARIETY OF WAYS

DavidPaul: The various ways that I hear God's Voice are like pieces to a puzzle. They are all valued, important, and necessary in my overall experience of wholeness, connection, and communication with God. One way of hearing this Voice isn't better than another. Depending upon the needs and circumstances of the moment, each form is perfect for the role that it plays.

For example, I still love sitting in silence, just basking in and feeling the peace of God within me. I can sit for hours in meditation, just *being* the Peace and Love that *I am*. In those moments, that's all I desire. No dialogue. No questions. *Just Being.*

Sometimes, however, I want something more specific in my communication with God. If I want guidance or reassurance on a particular issue, for example, and I'm not in a big hurry for the answer, I may ask for a sign. I don't need to know anything specific in that moment, and yet I'd love for some understanding or for an answer to unfold, so I ask for a sign.

Other times, especially when I'm challenged or frustrated with something and I want to get out of pain as soon as possible, I dialogue with this Inner Voice out loud. I acknowledge and voice my emotions and concerns and then ask for communication or a way to see things differently.

Communicating with God is like having an intimate relationship with someone. In intimate relationships, we connect, share, and communicate with one another in a multitude of different ways. We hold hands, kiss, cuddle, and develop special looks and gazes that mean something specific to one another. We write notes, cards, and emails. We give each other books to read or movies to watch. And, of course, we actually talk to each another. We have conversations. We share our hopes and dreams, and we counsel one another in times of need.

All of the ways that we communicate with one another are important and valuable in forming our overall experience of being in relationship. What would your life be like if you only hugged, kissed, and made love with your partner, but had no other communication together? Yeah, that might be perfect if you're a man in your early 20's! But that stage doesn't last forever because it's not ultimately fulfilling. What would it be like if you only watched movies or read books with one another, but little else? What if you had everything in your relationship except an actual, two-way conversation? If you're like me, you probably enjoy all forms of communication in the relationships you care about most. Why shouldn't it be the same in your relationship with God? Why not connect with God in as many ways as you can?

For me, hearing God's Voice as a conversational Voice is so richly rewarding that I can't imagine living without it at this point, but the fact is, *all of the ways* that I hear and connect with God are rewarding. They each offer something unique that the others do not. They each have a role to play in my overall experience of hearing God's Voice in the world. The more I integrate *all of them* into my life, the more fulfilling my experience of hearing and being God's Voice is.

DEVELOPING TRUST AND FAITH

DavidPaul: How does one come to trust that they are hearing God's Voice?

It's different for everyone—seven billion people, seven billion ways of coming to trust It. For Candace, it was very simple. She knew the words she heard were not her own. They were so loving, so kind, and felt so true that she immediately trusted their source.

For her, it has taken time, practice, faith, consistency, and more practice to be able to continue with that trust. Even if one has an experience like hers that was very opening and immediately offered trust, that trust has to be maintained, just as it does in any relationship. In the beginning of a relationship, two people usually start out trusting each other; they are innocent until proven guilty. That trust has to continually be earned, proven, honored, and respected throughout the length of the relationship. That is done one-sided or two. One can trust another regardless of what the other one does, and two parties may trust each other based on their actions and behaviors.

For Candace, the process of trust has continued with the opportunity to share this Voice with countless people and have them return each time saying, "Thank you. That rang so true," "Thank you. That was just what I needed to hear," or "Thank you. That was exactly right for me." As she continues to deliver messages that serve people, the trust is deepened and strengthened each time. In addition, the trust and faith are there each time Candace agrees to share this Voice, and every single time that she opens her mouth and that Voice comes through, that trust is reestablished and reconfirmed once again.

It is the same as being in relationship with anyone. In

some cases, trust may not be granted freely in the beginning. Trust may have to be earned from the start, and it may be that as one person engages in a relationship with the Holy Spirit, they ask God and the Holy Spirit to help them trust that Voice, the communication, and the consistency with which It is available to them, which is unending. They can ask for trust. They can pray for trust. They can hold a belief in trust within their heart and mind.

What often happens in a typical relationship is that trust is broken at some point. From one person's beliefs, thoughts, and understanding of the world to the other person's actions, words, deeds, miscommunications, or misunderstandings, confusion reigns and trust dissolves. That is the kind of relationship that people in the world are used to. It is as if one goes into any and all relationships with the understanding that eventually they will be burned. Eventually their trust will be broken. Eventually, somehow, this person will betray them or hurt them. That can only happen from one's thinking, and yet that is what will manifest it.

So when entering into a relationship with God, it is unlike any other relationship that one has ever entered into, though in Truth, one has never been out of that relationship. As one participates in that relationship, it is so unlike anything they have ever experienced because they will not be betrayed. They will not be burned. They will not be let down. The trust will not ever be compromised, and that, in and of itself, is something that is hard for many to fathom. It seems inconceivable, impossible, and why even dream about it when it is so unlikely.

What one must know entering into this relationship is that there can be nothing but trust. There can be nothing but Truth, Reality, clarity, and understanding, and as long as what you hear when you seek God's Voice is loving, caring, truthful, and real, you can know that God's Voice is speaking to you. If you hear something that is unloving, unkind, or untruthful, you can know that is not God's Voice talking to you. It is the same when you pick up the phone and the other person says 'hello' and you know who it is. It could be anyone calling and you know who it is from that one word. You recognize the voice. It is the same with God's Voice. You will come to recognize that Voice in such a way that there will be no doubt. There will be no confusion, and then the Words will only back up what you know, that this is loving, truthful, and real and therefore must be God's Voice.

It may start with little things. It may start with big elaborate communications. It doesn't matter. The more time you spend with that Voice, the more time you spend hearing, taking in, and applying what you hear, watching how your life benefits, seeing how your peace of mind grows, how your heart opens, and how your mind empties will all become proof for you that what you are hearing is God's Voice.

Trust is a tricky issue, and it all comes from within you, ultimately. If you can trust, you give that gift to *you*. It is not what you give to the other person. You do not trust them for their sake. You trust them for yours. In doing so, you will have a relationship that is trustworthy. Whatever belief you hold about what and who they are, that is what you will get.

You trust in the relationship. You trust in the Voice. You trust in the Holy Spirit's willingness and desire and passion to come to you. You trust that God wants to share Truth with you. You trust that this Voice is always available to you. You trust that It is loving and kind, and that is what you will receive. In any moment that it isn't, you stop, take a breath, and simply let go of whatever thoughts have been in your heart and mind just a moment before and reconnect with what you know is God. Reconnect with what you know is God's Voice. Ask that only God's Words come to you, then wait quietly and patiently for those Words to fill you.

DavidPaul: What is the difference between trust and faith?

One has the memory inside of them that they are One with God. It is because of that memory that one knows in their heart that God is. It is because of that memory that they believe in God, remember God, can hear God, and that God can hear them. It is innate because it *is* the Truth. You cannot take that Truth out of this aspect of God, which is to say, you cannot take God out of God. It is your inheritance. It is your heritage, and so It is yours.

Beyond that, you will have the thoughts that there is no God, you cannot hear God, and so forth—that is the ego doing its job and it does not change the basic Truth of what you are. The Truth of what you are does not change, nor can the ego ever take that away from you. So while you may have moments of confusion, the basic foundation is always there, and that is what drives you toward that connection.

The difference between trust and faith is that with trust, you believe, and with faith, you know. They are very similar but one is stronger. Faith is knowing that the person you are in relationship with is a Child of God. Even if you do not understand what they are doing or saying in that moment, you have faith, which is the memory and the awareness that the one in front of you is a Child of God, as are you, and that, in fact, they could not harm you in any way; they are not capable of it, nor are you capable of being harmed. When you take that faith out into the world, it is a constant reminder that though you may not be able to understand what is happening, you know it is perfect and that only what is right is unfolding.

PRACTICE

DavidPaul: For many years, we consciously joined with God's Voice every Sunday morning wherever we were. This became our primary time as a couple to officially turn off the phones, meditate, hear this Voice, and seek guidance. To better maintain our awareness of God's Presence throughout the week, we were eventually guided to "check-in" together at least once during the week as well.

With a regular practice of connecting in this way, the communications we received deepened and the messages would often build upon one another from one week to the next. We were frequently given homework assignments and tasks, and we would often share our "successes and failures" with one another and this Voice the following week. This practice of connecting with God's Voice on a regular basis greatly supported us in moving through many ingrained and dysfunctional patterns in our relationship and in our lives. The more we checked in, the more grace-filled our lives became.

If you don't consciously experience hearing this Voice in your life, be patient and keep trying. Developing more awareness of it could happen when you least expect it. It's different for everyone because we each seem to have our own unique set of thoughts and beliefs which keep us from hearing this Voice as we would like. For me, it took years of practice, persistence, and faith to finally open up to hearing this Voice within me. It is only now, after several years of hearing It, that I can honestly say that I *was* hearing this Voice all along and didn't know it. So even if you don't think you are hearing It, have faith that you *are* hearing this Voice in one way or another. Keep practicing and know that the more you choose to hear this Voice, the louder It becomes.

Joining with and hearing God's Voice is similar to exercise. You can talk about exercise all you want, but until you go to the gym and get on a machine, lift some weights, or start a class, nothing happens. It is the same with hearing this Voice for Love within you. You can talk about it all you want, and yet if you don't sit down and make that connection, it is only a theory. It is a tool that sits in the toolbox, though you can't remember where the toolbox is or whether you even have the tool, so it doesn't get used when you need it or want it.

As one engages with this Inner Voice more and more—through prayer, meditation, walking in the world engaged in conversation with this Voice, seeking guidance, direction, comfort, and union—this begins to build on itself and trust is gained in the relationship because it is unlike any other relationship one has experienced in the world.

It is difficult to conceive of and believe that, in fact, the Holy Spirit is part of you and cannot be separate from you. The Holy Spirit holds the deepest experience of Truth you are capable of having. As one walks around in the world, having come to believe that the Holy Spirit *is* their true Self, true Companion, true Guide, true Love, they will shine in that awareness. It will be this huge blushing that is so bright as to be overwhelming at times, and as a result, one will look upon another, whomever that may be in the world, and not be able to help but recognize God in the one across from them, the one behind them, the one to the left of them, and so on. It will be impossible to look out in the world at another and not see this Presence in front of you. Everywhere you look will be the Voice for God, and this is what you will acknowledge, recognize, and validate in the one in front of you because you cannot help it and that is what will come alive in them as a result. Everywhere you go, you will touch that part of them that you share with them because you are One with everyone who appears to be separate on the earth. You will come to understand and believe in the Oneness, and your only desire will be to acknowledge God's Voice in everyone you encounter because in so doing, the Oneness becomes stronger, more real, more aware, and a momentum builds that will eventually take over, and that is a ride you cannot wait to get on.

So little is asked of you while you venture off in this dream, but whatever is asked is only done so that you can fully remember and experience the Truth and the Joy of who and what you really are, and the Holy Spirit is waiting patiently, patiently, patiently within you to join you on that ride.

Chapter Summary

Hearing God's Voice is often shrouded in mystery and confusion because we experience being separate from God, when in Truth we are One. Allowing ourselves to hear God's Voice is a significant step in recognizing this Oneness because as we connect with God's Voice more and more, we eventually come to experience ourselves *as* God's Voice. Because this restoration of awareness *is* the purpose of this Voice within us, hearing God's Voice leads us into the experience of being the One, connecting with the One, in order to experience the One. It leads us into the recognition that we *are* Love, joining with Love, to experience our Self *as* Love.

The scope of "hearing God's Voice" is truly unlimited. It includes all forms of connection, perception, and experience of this Presence of Love that we are. It includes all forms of Self-experience and Self-realization, and it encompasses all of the physical senses of the body, as well as all of the spiritual senses beyond the body. Truly, everything can be an experience of hearing God's Voice with the Right-Perception. This is precisely why there are so many ways to hear God's Voice in the world.

The trick to hearing God's Voice then is to move our awareness out of the ego's thought system and into the quiet place within the mind where we are able to perceive this Presence within us. When our awareness is infused within the ego's thought system, we experience what we are not. When our awareness is restored to our Right-Mind, we experience the Truth and the Love that we *are*. In this State of Mind, God's Voice becomes our own, and we cannot help but think, speak, and create in Oneness with God and All That Is.

– 12 –

Wisdom from Over the Years

*Every kind thought you have ever had,
and every kind word you have ever spoken,
came from the Holy Spirit.*

When one first opens up to hearing God's Voice, it can be, as it was for Candace, a floodgate of communication coming in, or it can be a single word that delivers the message, or pieces of communication that are given here and there. Even though Candace's original experience resembled a floodgate, later, in learning how to put God's Words onto paper, it came very slowly and painstakingly. In the beginning, it was a word or a phrase, then a sentence, moving on to a paragraph, and finally a page would come through. This came about with practice, persistence, patience, and diligence, along with a sincere desire to hear and share God's Voice with herself and others. One way to share this Voice is to put It on paper and then pass the paper around.

EARLY ENTRIES FROM CANDACE'S NOTEBOOK

Candace: About a year after I began hearing God's Voice within me, I was guided to connect with this Voice every morning and write down the messages that I heard in a notebook. I hadn't written down any of the messages before then. I just listened to them within me. So when I first began the process of writing down the words I was hearing *as I was hearing them*, it started out as a rather slow and challenging exercise for me. But with every passing day, I got better at hearing, writing, and heeding the messages. Below are the first few entries from my notebook, which show my progression of writing these messages down, as well as the variety of things I heard.

June 23, 1995
Walk your talk....

June 24, 1995
Blue.
No one is at fault when one loses a game. (This comment was made in relation to feeing bad about something that happened the night before.)
The color blue is a message.
You are loved.... Know it. Feel it. See it. Speak it. Hear it. Love it. You are loved.
Amen.

June 25, 1995
Check in more often. Don't wait til later. It is with joy and ease that we have this communication today. It is through your willingness and surrender that this is happening.
You are lovely and delightful. You may heal yourself through joy, through hope, through failing to remember your sorrows, through victory over your shortcomings (perceived).

You are one who can know the Truth in all situations but can forget to ask. Trust the guidance you receive. Trust that the guidance you receive is True guidance. You know this in your heart. Settle into it, your heart, and make a place for yourself there. There is always room for you in your heart. Go there child. We love you.

Amen.

June 26, 1995

Yes, precious one, today we will move in a different direction. Today you will gather puzzle pieces of information from all those around you. You will gather information from all sources about the direction of your path. It will be up to you to recognize these pieces and make sense of them. Of course, we will help you. This is a lesson in seeing Source in everyone, in hearing Source in everyone, in knowing Source in everyone, in appreciating Source in everyone.

Get your notebook and begin.... We love you.

June 27, 1995

Aloha, precious one. Surrender deeper. Surrender to Truth, to Knowing, to Love, to Joy, to Peace, to Serenity. It is with Joy (God) that we may have this communication and experience for ourselves the delight in our joining. You did well getting the puzzle pieces yesterday. You also missed quite a few. (Happy face) We had fun. Enjoy, relax, and surrender into your heart's desire. It is there waiting for you and cannot be denied forever.

Amen.

June 28, 1995

Good morning child. Precious one, you are learning to be connected in every moment. When every experience is a possible puzzle piece to your joy and happiness, it keeps you

Continue to ask the question, "Why am I here?" and continue to get the answer. Let the answer guide you in your life and in your work.Everyone has a gift and a purpos, a mission to be performed for God and themselves. Become more and more aware of yours. It is time to begin to fulfill it.

much more interested. Does it not? You are waking up to your heart's desire. Keep surrendering to it.

Begin a second notebook. Let this be for your heart's desire and all that that would mean. Let your heart's desire pour out of you into the world to shine light on all your Brothers and Sisters. Bless them with your love. Bless yourself with this love. Go this day and be happy.

Amen.

BEING A MESSENGER

October 31, 1997

Greetings and blessings to you, precious one. This is a good way to start the day, is it not? Let's begin with a prayer for you to use for these sessions.

"God, may You help me and guide me in all that I do, that I may better work for You. Show me how to align our Wills through this and all that I do. Thank You, Father. Amen."

That was tougher than you thought it would be. Perhaps committing to yourself that you won't change anything you are given (meaning the Words of the Holy Spirit) even if it doesn't make sense to you, because it may just be that you are not ready to hear, though you may be someday. If you change it, it is gone forever. It won't be there for you when you need it. It is important to become very clear in your intention for this communication, and how you will receive it. What do you want to accomplish from this?

Candace: Clear communication with God. A friendship with God. The ability to be loving in every thought, word, and deed. A sense of Servantship that carries me through this lifetime. Peace in my Heart and Mind.

That is a good start. Then what state of Mind/Being would you need to be in to accomplish those goals from this work? Come to it in humility, grace and gratitude rather than thinking about getting it out of the way and getting on with other more important things. Is anything really more important than the goals you have listed here? I can think of nothing. Hold these goals in your mind each day when you begin this work with Us, so that you can be clear as to what is really important to you. Be reminded that nothing else actually matters. Not the laundry, the cleaning, the shopping, the work out, nothing. Only this will bring you peace. We sound like a commercial trying to sell you on a weight loss program, yet use your own discernment to determine what is true for you. We cannot do that for you. We can only state the Truth. Your free will determines what you do with the Truth. May it be with God's Blessings that you do what is truly best for you.

On with the session.... It would be very good to discontinue the use of the word 'channeling' in your description of what you do. Annie is Mary's Stenographer. What shall you be? A Messenger? "Please don't kill the messenger," they say. Perhaps that is why this title has scared you. You feel like a victim when you are the messenger, when, in fact, it is the position of least responsibility. You are not responsible for the message itself, only the delivery of it. You cannot be held accountable for the message. Isn't this a relief? It should be. Rejoice in this freedom, knowing that you have chosen this, you have asked for the opportunity to be a messenger, as there was nothing else you wanted more. Next time we will work on your worthiness for it.

Have a nice day. We love you Sister, and wish only the best for you. Please do not turn us off today, just because you turn this machine (computer) off.

The Holy Spirit and your Friend

WHY AM I HERE?

November 16, 1997

We love you precious one. We have always loved you; you know that. Be not afraid of these words that come to you in this way. Be not afraid to hear the Truth, for It serves you. Precious one, know that the Truth is in you. Who would you be without your story? A happy person? A contented person? One without the need to make bad choices, be self destructive, create drama? How about just one little soul who fulfills her destiny quietly, peacefully, lovingly, in communion with God—no frills, no glamour, no recognition? Would that be fun? Would it be enough to have a completely fulfilling relationship with God that no one else knew about—just you and God? Perhaps at that time you could teach others how you've done it. To share it before you have understood it, mastered it, accepted it, had it completely, is to give it away before you have owned it.

Be committed to complete ownership of this experience you have with God, then share it. This will come about in time and with practice and discipline. At this point you are still struggling to have this fully, still struggling with how best to use this Gift. It has been given to you to use for yourself, to hear God so that you can be guided in all situations, not just the obvious and easy ones. This Gift has been given to you to use and experience, then share. It has been given to you so that you can apply it to your life and show others how to do the same. You have had many lifetimes in which hearing God was not a possibility in your mind. You vowed to bring God's Voice into the world this lifetime and use It to the fullest, creating miracle after miracle with It, and in the process inspiring others to find their Voice for God within themselves.

When you do not use this Voice in your hours of need, you are, in fact, showing others that this Voice is only for the good times, not all times. You are saying that this Voice is only there for you when you are balanced and happy and able to hear It due to your state of being, rather than God's Voice being there for you always, especially when you are uncertain and afraid.

Continue to ask the question, 'Why am I here?' and continue to get the answer. Let the answer guide you in your life and in your work. You are here for a reason, as are all of God's children. All of His children want to know why they are here, what is their purpose, what is their gift, how do they use their gift to fulfill their purpose. They are only asking these questions because there are answers to them. Everyone has a gift and a purpose, a mission to be performed for God and themselves. Become more and more aware of yours. It is time to begin to fulfill it. We love you!

PEACE

December 8, 1997

Greetings precious one. Good morning. Today is a day of peace for you. A day that you can have to practice peace, perfect peace, being at peace with everything that happens. This means being one or joining with everything. Peace, just like paradise, is a state of being. You can have it anywhere, anytime, anyhow, under any circumstances. That is the beauty of it. You do not have to go anywhere or do anything. It is

As each one of God's children makes his or her way Home again, they are performing a beautiful dance along the way.... The practice of being in the moment and truly seeing the beauty and the grace of each step is the key.

just yours for the asking, seeking, taking, choosing. Choose peace. It is that simple. Peace over struggle. Peace over pain. Peace over disharmony. It is a tough choice, but you can do it. You can spend this day choosing peace in any and every situation. Peace with yourself, peace in your mind, peace in your interaction with others, peace in every situation. Practice this today and see how simple it really is. Believe it or not, this could become a habit—peace as a way of life.

You have the concept that peace is indifference or neutrality or not caring, but that is not so. It is acceptance, understanding, and a lack of judgment. This is a deep level of caring, a deep level of love. This is how God loves and how He maintains peace. So if peace came from unconditional love, would it then be worthwhile to love in this way? It would seem so. Practicing peace seems an easier place to begin than practicing unconditional love. Peace takes tremendous will power, for disharmony is what you are used to. Fortunately, peace is your natural state of being, so once it is regained, it is easy to maintain. It becomes easier to regain again and easier to maintain for longer, then even easier to regain, until finally, you are at peace for good.

All your little steps are taking you there. The way you are getting there looks different from the way your mate is getting there, but it is the same in Truth. You have each found ways that work for you, and each other's ways do not necessarily work for the other. So they might seem to each of you to not be working at all, when in fact, they are. This is the beauty of it. It is a dance, and a dance worth watching.

As each one of God's children makes his or her way Home again, they are performing a beautiful dance along the way. That is what keeps us entertained through all of this. Watching the dance is an honor, as it is a beautifully choreographed piece of art that is unfolding in complete Grace and Glory for all to see. The practice of being in the moment and truly seeing the beauty and the grace of each step is the key. Without that ability, it would sometimes appear to be a stumbling, bumbling lot of moves with no purpose or rhythm. This is why choosing to be present, to be in the moment, and to see through the Eyes of Love and Peace can be so worthwhile. Choose this precious one, and see, truly see, what happens.

We love you.

ROLL IN THE MUD

February 6, 1998

Greetings precious one. What a glorious day. The heavens have opened up and are blessing you with all of their riches. (It is raining cats and dogs outside.) Just imagine opening your heart and receiving an equivalent amount of Love from God. It *is* possible, and sometimes just as messy. You notice that it is not messy when it leaves the heavens, only when it hits the earth. Why is that? Perhaps the rain is washing away all of the dirt that has accumulated. Perhaps God's Love is washing away all of the Earth-Mind Consciousness that has built up. And in the process of washing away, it looks ugly for a little while. Soon it will be beautiful again, and sooner still it will become dirty.

Often, one tries to keep something clean and pristine by not using it, thinking that by keeping something in a box or on a shelf it will be preserved. This is to deny oneself the experience of that thing, only later to find that it has been ruined by sitting in a box or on a shelf, and that it would have kept longer if it had been used. Many times things improve with use, especially if they are used lovingly. This "thing" or "it" in this case, is one's life. Therefore, do not live cautiously for fear of getting dirty. Live dangerously. Roll in the mud. Play a lot. Mess up your hair. Lose buttons. And know that you get

... do not live cautiously for fear of getting dirty. Live dangerously. Roll in the mud. Play a lot. Mess up your hair. Lose buttons. And know that you get out of your life whatever you put into it.

out of your life whatever you put into it.

Blessings to you. Amen

HOLY UNION

February 20, 1998

Precious one, a holy union is a sacred trust. A holy union is different than a union. A holy union means that two people have joined together with God and have agreed to do God's Will in their partnership. The purpose of a holy union is joining with God. You have entered into a holy union, and as such there are responsibilities that go along with this. There is a responsibility to yourself and your partner to experience God in yourself and your partner. There is also a responsibility to experience God in all things so that you may someday know only Love. Your goal in this lifetime is to be only Love. It is therefore essential that you join in holy union so you may come to know and love your self as no other. The most important work you could do this lifetime would be to come to know and love yourself. It is from this that you may know and love another. To live as though everyone on earth were simply a reflection of you would be the highest form of living.

You have fears that you will not measure up as a partner. The person you need to be a partner to is yourself. You cannot fail in your partnership with DavidPaul. You can only fail in your partnership with yourself. Fortunately, you cannot fail in your partnership with God either. God's experience of your partnership is Perfection. This could be your experience as well. Indeed to know and to love your self is to know and love God, and to feel God's Presence in your heart and mind. This is the ultimate in living.

We love you and bless you in every way.

IN TOUCH

Candace: People submit questions to the Holy Spirit through our website, and we answer these questions with the Holy Spirit and then post the replies. One day, someone who disagreed with the content of our website asked if we were really "in-touch" with the Holy Spirit. The person also asked us to prove our connection by telling him his middle name. After reading his e-mail, we received the following communication.

August 1, 1999

Greetings and blessings to you precious ones. Indeed it is a joyous occasion to gather together with you in this way. There are so many reasons for the messages that you would receive via email. Part of those reasons may include validation or recognition. It also includes for you the opportunity to look into any places within yourselves where you have a matching experience with the person who writes to you. So if someone like Joseph asks, "Are you in touch with the Holy Spirit?" you can ask yourself that question, "Am I in touch with the Holy Spirit?"

The question for him is, "Why is it that *you* doubt *your* connection to the Holy Spirit?" He cannot doubt *your* connection unless he doubts *his* own connection.

The two of you can also take this opportunity to find a place within yourselves where this may be true to whatever degree. When we join together in this way, there is a connection with this Voice, of course, and yet in your day-to-day, hour-to-hour, moment-to-moment life, how connected are you? Are you in touch with the Holy Spirit? That is his question, and it simply offers you an opportunity to look deeper into yourselves, to ask certain questions, and to join ever deeper in your communion with God.

No physical reactions occurred inside Candace when she

read that letter from Joseph, where normally her heart might stop for a moment, or she might get a knot in her stomach. None of these things occurred. It was that person's experience, and it is not her experience of the Holy Spirit. And she did not even have to react to this projection. At the same time, still ask yourself, "Are there any places within me where I doubt my connection? Am I in touch?"

You will be challenged. The more that you put yourselves out there, the more you will be challenged to prove it, the more people will come along and say, "Tell me my middle name," as if the Holy Spirit were a psychic. Obviously, there's no need to go there. You are not out to prove anything. At the same time, you want to prove to yourselves your connection with the Holy Spirit, your worthiness for this connection, and your ability to apply this connection under any circumstances. One of Candace's dreams in having this connection was that the whole entire world could come crumbling down around her and she would stand there like a rock and say hello to the Holy Spirit first, not run, not scream, not cry, not panic, but first say hello to God, to have that connection under the worst of circumstances, to tune-in first and panic later if need be.

Where within you would you not do that first? As you put yourselves out there more and more, and as you consider writing books and sharing the communication that you've received, you will receive criticism. You can do whatever you want with this criticism. You can learn from it. You can know yourself better. You can project it back on to the person who gave it to you. You can bless that person for showing you a place within you that you can explore more thoroughly. You can love that person where they are.

There are many, many options, and you will be faced with this over and over again. You each already know the one response, to be loving to whomever this is occurring. If you cannot do that, then there is no walking the talk of this teaching. In that moment, be loving to the person who seems to be attacking you or ask the Holy Spirit why it is happening. Ask, "What can I do to shift this?" or be loving in that moment and walk away and ask later. If you say, "I'm so angry about this and I know the truth of what's really gone on!" you are angry with that person because they have told you something you did not want to hear.

Do either of you (Candace or DavidPaul) have any questions?

DavidPaul: Why don't You play prove it with people?

Faith is something that you have. Faith is a desire, a desire to believe. And what you believe *is*. A lack of faith is wanting to not believe. So how many things would you have to say and do to prove to somebody to completely shift and transform them to a place where they become filled with faith? You could spend the rest of your life on one person. They will create what they need to create to develop faith or not. Your job is not to instill faith in them. That is between them and God. Your job is to offer them communication, and it is not to prove to them that they should have faith because this is real or not real. That is *their* life lesson. It may be ten lifetimes or a thousand lifetime lessons. It could not possibly be your job to do that for someone else. Can you see that? Telling someone their middle name would just be a party trick. It has no value. It has no substance. It will not prove anything.

DavidPaul: So what would a good response to him be?

What I told Candace this morning what his middle name was, "One who lacks faith." And she was told not to apologize for anything. She wanted to say, "I'm sorry that you're not happy with the response. I'm sorry that you are unable to experience

The most important work you could do this lifetime would be to come to know and love yourself. It is from this that you may know and love another. To live as though everyone on earth were simply a reflection of you would be the highest form of living.

faith," or whatever it may be. There are no sentences that are to begin with, "I'm sorry," in this situation. You can speak honestly and straightforwardly to this one and say that as he stated, he is comfortable with his current situation and until the pain and the suffering truly becomes unbearable, he is not motivated to change it. Does that make sense?

DavidPaul: Yeah.

You can see the benefit to so many people contacting you with their communications, and they are just you in drag, offering you the opportunity to explore in yourselves things that you may take for granted with regard to the Holy Spirit, places you may not want to go, questions you may not want to ask, fears you may not want to acknowledge, doubts you may not want to admit. And these people will offer all of those to you, everyone last one of them and then some. And that is the beautiful gift that they are.

God's Puzzle

November 18, 1999

It is not life experience that teaches a baby to laugh. She is born with a spark of God, and that part of her remains intact. She is whole in her totality, though God is incomplete without her. This is why each one of His children (sparks of Himself) must return to Him eventually to complete the Giant Puzzle that is Source, and in doing so, each piece will finally feel its completeness. What a happy day that will be. And yet, through the perceptions in one's mind, it would be possible to experience this completeness as having already happened because, in Truth, it has.

If each of God's children must return to Him to complete

the Puzzle, is it not true that you are a piece of that Puzzle? Is it not also true then that you have a vested interest in that Puzzle being completed? Does it do you any good to hurry back to Source when nothing can be accomplished until all of the pieces are in place? Is it true then that what would do you the most good would be to help the most amount of God's children return Home? This is the way to live.

If what benefits the whole ultimately benefits you, then serve the whole. And do it lovingly and humbly, knowing that you are only really serving yourself. You are not doing anyone else any favors in Truth. Your call to service, then, is to serve yourself and you do this best by helping everyone along the way get to the same destination with as much Grace and dignity as possible. Can you do this? Are you doing this? How can you do this better?

Is it not essential then to slow down and see where you could serve yourself at every opportunity? Slow down so that you can notice when you are being called to service. Service can be as small as a smile or as big as a loving thought. It only matters that you are able to be of service to those who are trying to get Home, and that you know you are doing it for yourself rather than for the other person so that there are no debts incurred in the process. How can you do this better? Be aware of this question, asking yourself continually, how can I do this better?

AOL STOCK

January 17, 2000

Greetings and blessings to you, precious ones. Indeed it is a joyous occasion to gather together with you in this way, having church. For Candace, your mind is filled with thoughts and possibilities, potential outcomes. Yes, it is very important for you to be in your own business. You do not have to save anyone or anything, nor are you responsible for anyone or anything other than yourself. Be in your business, allowing the rest of the business to be God's.

Do you have questions you would like to ask?

DavidPaul: The AOL Time Warner stock deal. (DavidPaul works at AOL) Obviously there is stuff going around in the press that we won't be an Internet company anymore and the stock won't go up as quickly.

It does not matter what occurs with AOL Time Warner, or iPlanet, or anyone else. What matters in your movie is your faith in being able to manifest your dreams and in overcoming your fears. Does that make sense?

DavidPaul: It is just so hard.

That is the point. We have said previously that between now and living your dream you will overcome your fears. Your goal is to walk away fearless because you know that God is taking care of you. If you think that AOL and what they do is taking care of you, then you are misguided. It is not that you don't love and appreciate AOL and keep them in your prayers. It's only to know and have faith that God is taking care of you. You have said your prayers, made your statement to the universe, and have made a commitment to be a holy family. Between now and that time, all you are doing is letting go of fears. If you have the opportunity now to be complete with your work in two years, it is because you are making progress with your fears and for no other reason. It is not because there was a merger.

In your movie, your life and everything that happens in it is based on your writing and your directing. As you grow in strength, grow in faith, grow in certainty that what you are asking for is in your highest good and for the highest good of everyone involved, and you know in your heart that God is blessing that, then you can let go of what is between you and that prayer. That is all you would need to live your dream and be a holy family, and yet, you can't get there with the fears and lack of faith. For you to walk away from your company with enough money to live your dream and to have not overcome these issues would be pointless. Having your peace and your happiness come from the numbers in your bank account, having your faith be in a company, or having your security lie in the stock market, you can see that you would never have peace. This is an opportunity for you to deepen and strengthen your faith, your commitment, your prayers, your desires. That part is your responsibility.

It is important, essential, and the only thing that matters, the only thing that is True, the only thing that is Real, to believe in God. Yes, you still validate your company and you show up every day, but that is different than putting your faith, literally your faith in your future, into a company. You can have faith in that company and keep that company in your prayers and in God's Hands knowing that it is the symbol you are using, but your faith has to be in God. So you override the news and the talk at work, and for whatever comes, you give thanks.

DavidPaul's lesson of the week: Merger.... "Thanks, God." Stock goes down.... "Thanks God." Lots of fear.... "Thank you, God. I have the opportunity to work on fear." Lots of celebration.... "Thank you, God. I have the opportunity to celebrate this next step toward living my dream, which is really a step in deepening my faith in God." Whatever comes.... "Thank you, God." It is all in God's Hands, and your faith in God is what will allow you to leave AOL and pursue your dreams, not your faith in AOL.

Anything could happen to AOL; nothing could happen

to God. If something were to happen to AOL and you have faith in God and your prayers and desires, God will take care of you. Only something better can happen. It is putting the cart before the horse. You cannot trust this process until you can trust this process, and yet that is the point of this process. We will work on this over and over and over again. There will come a time when you will be as free of this as one can be, so that even when you become burdened by this, you will know it is just your lack of faith in God rather than an earthly fear. To put your faith in AOL is to build your house on sand. To have your faith in God and use AOL as a symbol is to build your house on rock.

CHAPTER SUMMARY

We each hear what we need to hear in order to awaken, and this Voice within us will speak to each of us right where we are to accomplish this. Do not worry if what you hear within you is different than what another hears. You need your message, and they need theirs. Be patient with this process, and know that whatever you hear and however you hear is absolutely perfect for you.

If each of God's children must return to Him to complete the Puzzle, is it not true that you are a piece of that Puzzle? Is it not also true then that you have a vested interest in that Puzzle being completed? Does it do you any good to hurry back to Source when nothing can be accomplished until all of the pieces are in place? Is it true then that what would do you the most good would be to help the most amount of God's children return Home?

– Part Three –

Choosing the Voice for Love

The Light that I am lights your way,
which lights my way, which lights your way,
which lights my way.

– 13 –

Seeking Your Inner Voice

*How I see is a choice. I can see the
world or I can see Heaven, and
the scenery doesn't change.*

When one seeks God's Voice in the world, they are
seeking Truth. They are seeking a perspective
that is Right-Minded and offers a way of seeing things
from a new light. When one seeks God's Voice in the
world, they give themselves the opportunity to see
things from a perspective that offers them peace,
joy, and the reminder of who they truly are. They give
themselves the gift of seeing the world through God's
Eyes—in whatever way and to whatever degree they
are willing. The Words they hear may sound different
to each one, and yet they will be given Truth every
time.

Hearing God's Voice has the potential to bring us peace when we are in pain, clarity when we are confused, and understanding when we do not know. Over the years, we have received countless questions from visitors to our website asking God for communication and guidance in times of need. Because we each have a unique set of thoughts, beliefs, and experiences, God will answer our questions right where we are knowing full well the thoughts and beliefs we are presently holding, what it is we are truly seeking, and what we are willing to hear. Ten people could ask the same question, and God could provide ten different answers. Each person is given whatever perspective or guidance they personally need on their path. It can be helpful to remember this when we listen to the guidance and communication that other people receive in their lives.

Below are a few examples of the types of questions people have submitted to us over the years. As you will see, no matter what we seek, this Voice for Love and Truth within gives us whatever insight and communication we need to remember the Truth of who we are and the Love our Father has for us.

FEAR OF A BROKEN HEART

Maggie: I am in the process of getting divorced and have met a very wonderful man who touches my soul. I am scared of a relationship because of a fear of not being perfect, and my main fear is that of a broken heart. I am wondering how this relationship will work out and how I should handle it so that no feelings will be hurt. I want to be with this man. Will I be? Will it be a forever relationship? Thank you.

Greetings and blessings to you precious one. You ask how to have this relationship without any feelings being hurt. Well, you will have to roll yourself up in cotton batting, lock yourself up in a closet and not have contact with anyone or anything, and then not allow your mind to think any thoughts. Perhaps then, with a little luck, you may not have your feelings hurt, and yet, even that is probably not possible.

So, with the prospect of beginning a relationship, what you must do is expect and look forward to the opportunity to have your feelings hurt so that you can come to know yourself better, know the areas where you are challenged, and pray that those places become healed, whole, and filled with faith and love rather than fear, as they are now. To have a fear of your heart breaking will allow you first and foremost to focus on your heart breaking rather than to focus on your heart opening and allowing more love, more joy, and more capacity for love to be within you.

The fear of a broken heart is what will create a broken heart. Nothing else can actually do it. You can be abandoned, abused, violated, unloved, rejected, and none of that need cause you to have a broken heart; it is how you handle the situation that will or will not cause you to experience having a broken heart. You can also have lots of love, support, and kindness in your life and still walk around believing that your heart is broken or will be broken. It is strictly your perspective and your experience of this situation that will cause you to have a broken heart or not.

To want to be with this man is one thing and to have it be what is best for you may be something different altogether. For you, the most important thing is to pray only for that which is in your highest good and to avoid the prayers that specifically ask to be with this person forever. You cannot focus on or worry about the future. It is something that is ever-changing based on your own evolution and where you are in your life. Something may be perceived as forever and then you could shift your perspective in an afternoon and change the course of your life entirely. The future is not important; it is the *now* that is important. How do you perceive *now*? How do you

.... with the prospect of beginning
a relationship, what you must do
is expect and look forward to the
opportunity to have your feelings hurt
so that you can come to know yourself
better, know the areas where you are
challenged, and pray that those places
become healed and whole and filled
with faith and love rather than fear....

love *now*? How open are you *now* to that which is for your highest good? Allow yourself to pray for peace and openness within your own heart so that you can receive and give love in the ways that you truly desire. That is your birthright, and if you truly want it, it will be done.

Blessings to you precious one. Amen.

Am I Doing the Right Thing?

Joanne: My fiancé and I just broke up, and I need to know if this was the right thing to do or not. I love him more than anything else in the whole world. We were planning on being married in April. I just felt like he put himself above me in his priorities. He would make plans with me and then go play golf instead, or he would simply forget to call because something more important came up. I love him and miss him very much, but I feel like maybe it's best for us to be apart until he can change this selfish aspect of his personality. Should I be patient and stick it out or move on?

Greetings and blessings to you precious one. To say that this person has a tendency to be selfish and to have the idea that you can change his personality, or that *he* can, is perhaps not very realistic. What is more realistic in making a lifetime commitment to someone is to make a commitment to who that person is in their entirety, to accept the things about them that you cannot change, and even different than that, to accept everything about them as potentially something that can never be changed—that who you know and see before you now is the person you will spend everyday of your life with. It is important to marry who is standing in front of you today and to not marry them for who you think they will become or to not marry them for who you are afraid they might turn into. It is the one in front of you who is real and who you would be spending your days with.

If you cannot live with the selfishness of this person now, it may only be magnified over days, weeks, months, or years in a marriage. Can you imagine yourself in this relationship with these tendencies multiplying over time? Or can you see yourself making peace with this and not having this person's selfishness impact you? Are you strong enough to not be affected by this person's selfishness? Or would you rather make a lifetime commitment to someone who does not have selfish tendencies? If this person is selfish with you, what will they be like with your family, your children, or over a lifetime?

This is an opportunity for you to do some soul-searching. If you experience this person as selfish, in what ways does his selfishness make you uncomfortable because you are selfish? What kinds of things about yourself would you like to change? What types of things about you would you like to experience differently? In what ways would you like to be different in a relationship? It is important for you to focus on you and to focus less on this person, their flaws, and the changes that they should make. Take this time to focus on you. What shifts can you make so that you like you better? In doing so, you will come to like yourself in such a way that you will attract and keep someone who equally likes themselves and who is equally committed to knowing themselves and working toward being the best person they can be.

Have faith that this process is one that is serving you in every way. Blessings to you precious one. Amen.

OVERCOMING ADDICTION

Cheryl: I am having trouble letting go of an over the counter addiction and smoking. I really need the Holy Spirit to guide me and strengthen me so I can overcome these things.

Greetings and blessings to you precious one. To want to give up the addictions you are speaking of is, of course, the first and biggest step. To know that there are things that you are doing that are not serving you is the most important awareness that can happen to shift addictions. At the same time, it creates pain because you suddenly become aware that this is not something that is serving you, and yet you are still doing it. There is a time lag between the awareness that what you are doing is causing you pain and the inability to stop doing it. Know that once you get to the other side, there will be tremendous peace, and yet you can still have peace in this process knowing that your awareness has taken you to the first and the biggest step in changing something you are unhappy with.

There will be a time when these addictions will be behind you and you will have the blessing of addiction in your experience and the strength and the confidence that comes from overcoming it. You will then be able to encourage and inspire others as well. This transition period is painful, confusing, paradoxical, and at the same time exciting and door opening.

It is important to be patient, loving, and kind and accepting with yourself right now. Battling, fighting, and abusing yourself to give up something such as an addiction is not the best way, although it is often the most common way. Be patient and kind and know that for you, the more that you love yourself, the more you can let go of these things that do not serve you.

Spend time each day consciously noticing, admiring, and loving yourself. Think about what you like about you, what makes you special, what you want to share with others, and what you wish others knew about you. Focus on those things and experience them within your heart and mind. Experience the love that you have for yourself. You do have tremendous love within you, though for you it is just buried, confused, and doubtful at times. Underneath all of that, there is a very deep and abiding love that you have for you. That love is what will carry you through this process.

The more you love yourself, the more you cannot do the things that do not serve you. The more you love you, the less room there is for anything other than that which is good. Spend more time loving you and there will be less room for these addictions. It is truly that simple. Eventually, you will run out of room within you to do those things that do not serve you. Love yourself and have faith that this day is coming.

Blessings to you precious one, Amen.

My Fairy Tale is Gone

John: My girlfriend and I recently split up. I called her a few days ago and she said that it was over, that I had gotten on her nerves to the point where she didn't see any point in communicating with me anymore—ever. I told her I was completely devastated. She said, "I know, but that happens to people everyday and you need to act like an adult for once."

I just don't understand what happened. I am so hurt and confused and lonely. I bought her flowers almost every week we dated and treated her like a princess. I cry and pray every day for her to return. How can I get my fairy tale back?

Greetings and blessings to you, precious one. What is attractive about a person is their character, their strengths, their goals, their beliefs. In some cases, it may be external things, and yet, for the most part, it is who they are and all of the richness they bring into the world and share with another. That is what you brought to this relationship in the first place. Who you became over time was a person who is in love

What is more realistic in making a lifetime commitment to someone is to make a commitment to who that person is in their entirety, to accept the things about them that you cannot change, and even different than that, to accept everything about them as potentially something that can never be changed....

with this other person, rather than a man of character, virtue, ideas, and goals. You lost who you were in the process of this relationship, and you lost what made you desirable to her in the first place.

You have not done anything wrong or bad. This happens naturally for people in relationships when they are not strong and certain about who they are and about their character and strengths. Those become lost in the course of a relationship. For you, it would be best to allow your fairy tale to read onto the next page where it says, "And they lived happily ever after. The End." You close the book and say, 'That was a nice story. God bless those characters.' And you move on.

Give thanks in your heart for having known this person and for having learned that in the course of falling deeply and wonderfully in love, you lose yourself. Then go about your life, without this person, rediscovering your strengths, your character, your virtues and goals. Focus on these and strengthen these. They are already instilled within you in a very deep way. Make contact with those things on the deepest level that you can, so that you bring them into the world and into your relationships, rather than bringing your neediness, your dependence, or your suffering, which came as a result of losing yourself in this relationship.

Rediscover within you all of these things. When you feel strong and confident in who you are, bring that into the world and allow another relationship to unfold in your life, being mindful not to lose yourself in the process. It is not to be self-centered when you step into a relationship, but to continue to make yourself, your relationship with God, and your family, work, goals, and priorities as important as they truly are.

You have everything within you that you need to accomplish this. It is only for you to make the decision and take the time to do this. Allow yourself to be motivated to maintain who you are and to allow your partner to maintain who they are so that the relationship becomes the blessing of the gifts that you each bring, knowing that you are stronger as a couple than the sum of your parts.

Blessings to you on this happy venture. Amen.

A SECRET TO SHARE

Maria: I have been through a lot over the last 3 years. I have divorced, suffered from cancer, and started a new relationship with someone I care a great deal about. One of my problems is that I have been trained professionally to be a very secretive person. I have kept things and told lies to this person because of my secretiveness. Needless to say, it has created problems in this relationship. I know that this is wrong, but when you are trained this way, it is a hard habit to break. I worked undercover for several years so you can see where this is coming from. I don't want to be like this. Please pray for me and give me some insight as to how I can break this habit. Thank you.

Greetings and blessings to you precious one. Indeed it is a joyous occasion to gather together with you in this way. Thank you for your request of prayers and guidance.

It is one thing to say that your secretiveness comes as a result of the work you have done, but it may be true that you chose the work you did out of a desire to be secretive. Which came first, the chicken or the egg? In your case you have been protecting yourself and doing your best to avoid being hurt any more than you have already been hurt. You have created the idea that to be secretive, to close down, or to hide is the best way you know to protect yourself. This keeps you from letting someone in, and it keeps you from being able to come out. There is the fear that if one were to know you completely, they would not like you or love you. There is the fear that if

The more you love you, the more you cannot do the things that do not serve you. The more you love you, the less room there is for anything other than that which is good. Spend more time loving you and there will be less room for these addictions. It is truly that simple.

you love or that if you are loved, you will ultimately be hurt.

There are many ways to experience life's lessons. Every experience can teach you something, yet the same experience might teach ten people ten different things. If one reaches into their oven to take something out and they are burned, one person might say that reaching into a hot oven will cause you to be burned. Another person would say to use your oven mitts when reaching into a hot oven to prevent getting burned. Another person may decide that baking is dangerous and they give it up altogether. Some people might think that they had been stupid and deserved to be burned. You can see that the same experience can offer people many different conclusions. You have had certain experiences and based on those you came to believe that it is better to hide and better to not love or be loved. Those conclusions do not need to be your truths any longer.

The real truth is that it is not safe to *not* love or be loved because if you do not love or are not loved, surely you will perish. If you think it is better to hide so that one cannot know you and have the opportunity to not like you, you also close the door to the opportunity for someone to like you for who you really are. The key here is for you to break the "habit" of not liking yourself and being afraid to love yourself. You are a very good and sweet and loving being. You are a beloved daughter of God. Would you tell God that any of His children are unlikable or unlovable? You would not and could not because you know that this is not true.

Spend some time each day contemplating what you can do every day, what tiny step you could take that day toward liking yourself and loving yourself. Eventually you will look forward to the opportunity to be honest, to the opportunity to put yourself out there. Eventually you may go to the one you are in relationship with now and say to him honestly, "I am sorry I have not been truthful. I did not know that I was afraid that you might not like what you found and I did not know that I was afraid to love and be loved. I want to like who I am. I want to share that with you, and I want to learn to love and be loved." You have everything you need to be able to make that statement and mean it.

Know that God's Voice is within you at all times. All you need do is go inside yourself and ask that you be aware of your connection with this Voice, and it will be done. Know that you can ask for anything and that all guidance and direction will be given to you. You are very loved indeed. Whether it frightens you or not, you are very loved indeed.

Blessings to you, precious one. Amen.

FINDING A LIFE PARTNER

Lisa: I'm 35 years old and ready to open my heart to a true partner. I have honored myself in the past by leaving relationships that weren't right, yet I wonder if my idea of how I think it is supposed to be is preventing me from creating what I truly want. I don't want to settle.

I met a man recently and was very excited after our first date, but on our 2nd date, he seemed more excited about the possibility of sex than having a relationship. Do you have any insight that would give me more peace in this part of my life?

Greetings and blessings to you precious one. Indeed, it is a joyous occasion to gather together with you in this way. Thank you for your letter and for your request.

It is important to not have too many ideas about how a spiritual partnership should look. One cannot know what is best for them and can only open up to allowing the universe to partner them with the right person. There is not one particular person that is a soul mate to you. That is the bad news. The good news is that most of the men on the planet *could* be a soul mate to you when you truly become ready.

To have the relationship that you want, it is as if you become ripe and ready to be plucked from being single, learning, growing, experiencing, and questioning. You become ripe for relationship. At the same moment that you become ripe, someone else on the planet will become ripe, and your paths will cross.

There are many degrees of ripeness. You have crossed paths with some when you were unripe and so were they, and yet there was an attraction drawing you together. This was a process of learning and growing, so that you could become ripened and ready for plucking. You are still in that process and are very near to being ripe. It is now truly a matter of making a very deep decision. "Now *is* the time, and *I am* open and ready to do this." Then nothing will keep you from it. Then you have to get out of the way and allow the universe to set you up with the matching partner.

It is one thing to have a list of requirements, and it is another thing to have faith in your Creator to match you up in full knowingness with the right partner for you, the one who will give you what it is you are truly seeking, which is growth, development, evolution, peace, love, happiness, distress, challenge, and everything that will give you your ultimate goal.

Perhaps this person will not be in the package you have anticipated or may have issues that are very challenging. Perhaps that is the point, and perhaps not. Do not take the next person who steps into your life to be this life partner, but instead allow yourself to become fully ready, fully ripened. When the time comes and this person steps into your life, you will know it. You will not have doubts.

There is much that you are open to, and there are fears

When you feel strong and confident in who you are, bring that into the world and allow another relationship to unfold in your life, being mindful not to lose yourself in the process. It is not to be self-centered when you step into a relationship, but to continue to make yourself, your relationship with God, your family, your work, your goals, and your priorities as important as they truly are.

as well. Your worst fears will happen whether you are with someone or not, if that is the state of your mind. It is important to become willing to risk your worst fears and then find the freedom on the other side. Examine your fears. Experience them. Try them on. Share them with others. Learn to laugh at them. Play the game of asking, "What is the worst that can happen? And when that happens, what would be the worst that can happen?" Take it to the end and see that whatever happens is not the end of the world. It is just something that happens.

There are many countless rewards in receiving a life partner. Countless does not begin to describe it, and yet becoming a life partner is even more rich. That is the process you are in now. Continue this unfolding of yourself, your heart, your mind, your fears, your dreams, and allow yourself to truly become ready, truly become open, and to know that all good things will be given to you as a result. You need not fear being alone forever, yet that is one of your fears to examine. Many gifts lay ahead of you, and it is important to be open to them so that you do not miss them on your journey.

Blessings to you precious one. Amen.

An Empty Feeling Within Me

Shannon: I am a 27 year old wife and mother of two beautiful girls, ages two and four, yet I still have this empty feeling within me. I have a lot to be thankful for and have a terrific family but still there is a void. I have gone through years of my life dealing with cancer in my family. My grandfather passed away almost 7 years ago from cancer, and my life just doesn't seem to be the same. My father then got prostate cancer only to be followed by a brain aneurism. Then my husband got testicular cancer to be followed by my grandmother with breast cancer. What do I do?

Greetings and blessings to you precious one. Indeed, it is a joyous occasion to gather together with you in this way. Thank you for your letter and for your request.

Indeed, you have had many challenges within your family. It is important to remember that these types of challenges are most often wake up calls. They are calls to those who are afflicted and to those who love them, to wake up in whatever ways one might be asleep. If any of those with cancer or any of those who love them have been seeking more faith, more awareness of God, a deeper, richer experience of God, a deeper appreciation for life, for nature, for family, for relationship, for those things that truly matter, often times a life threatening illness will do just that.

If one has prayed for a richer experience of their life on earth, what better way than to be on the verge of losing it to appreciate it fully? You say there is a void within you, and perhaps this void is God. For you, despite how many life-threatening illnesses you are surrounded by, there is still a void where God is concerned. That in and of itself is a wake-up call. Each time there is something before you, such as an illness or a physical condition that threatens one's life, that is the time to stop what you are doing and join with God. That is the time to pray. That is the time to ask God to join you in your heart and mind and bring you comfort, peace, and the knowing that regardless of what happens, everything is ok.

You have so many opportunities and inspirations to join with God and now is the time to do that. Stop whatever you are doing, and join with God. Stop what you are doing and pray. Look around you and see what you have. It is so easy to focus on what you have lost and what you are losing and what you might lose, and now it is time to turn 180 degrees and become aware of what you have. Become aware of the richness and gifts and people and joy and beauty and grace in your life on a day to day basis. You have the laughter of your precious little daughters and the joy on their faces when you play with them. You have the witnessing of their learning and unfolding. You have the pleasure of a loving family. You have the beauty of all that is in front of you. There is so much richness, and yet the focus is on loss. You can see that what one focuses on becomes their reality.

Perhaps the void is that you have turned your back on what is good and beautiful and wonderful and amazing in your world. It already exists. It is already there. You are just facing the other way. When you turn around you will see all of the beauty and the grace that you already have. It is so easy to turn away from the good in one's life when the focus is on tragedy. In what ways do you gain by focusing on tragedy? In what ways do you lose by turning away from the Life in your life?

You have these two beautiful children brimming over with Life, and yet they cannot outweigh the tragic. Each of these experiences is your opportunity to join with God, to deepen your faith, to look around and see what you *do* have, to appreciate each moment, including waking up in the morning, your family, your home, the ways you laugh, learn, play, struggle, and are challenged by on a day to day basis, and to deepen the gratitude you have for the wind and the rain and the sun and the snow and everything in between. It is a wake-up call. The ones in your life who have become sick have given you the gift of this opportunity of a wake-up call. Now it is time to wake up. The alarm is going off.

Blessings to you, precious one. Amen.

CHAPTER SUMMARY

When we experience pain in our lives, it is because we are not feeling the Love that we truly *are* in any given moment. We are experiencing the thoughts of the ego that would try to convince us who we are not. By recognizing that we are in pain and bringing this pain to this Presence of Love within us for healing, understanding, or guidance, we release our identification with those limiting thoughts, and we empower ourselves to reclaim our true Identity.

Because this Voice for Love within us has only Love to offer us, listening to our Inner Voice will teach us how to love our Self as God loves us. It will also teach us how to Love the rest of our Self that we perceive in the world. Know that everything you see in yourself and in the world is a reflection of your mind—a reflection of your thinking—and *all of it* can be used, with this Voice for Love within you, as an opportunity to know and love yourself more fully.

– 14 –

Fulfilling Your Life's Purpose

*The Light of God in me rekindles the
Light in all of God's children.*

Hearing God's Voice is more than hearing words being spoken to you. It is the opportunity to live a life where your purpose is understood. Hearing God's Voice is the opportunity to bring meaning to your life and understanding to your experiences. God's Voice can be for you a way of life, a way to live in the world with Truth rather than beautiful words you hear on occasion. Though the words may be lovely, it is what you do with them that matters.

THE MEANING AND PURPOSE OF LIFE

Candace: I know you've talked about this before, but can you tell us again what the purpose of life is?

Most people walk around in the world feeling at least a little bit unfulfilled, unsatisfied, and wondering what their purpose is or what is the meaning of life. The meaning of life is to give you the opportunity to remember the Truth of who you really are, and your purpose is the same, and through remembering that, you remind another. That is your true purpose.

It seems that each of God's children in the world has at least some awareness that something is missing or incomplete. They look for completion in a partner, child, job, or thing, and yet even with all of that, there is still a sense that something is missing. This something is their connection to the One Child of God and their relationship with their Creator.

When one perceives themselves as separate and perceives another as "the enemy," it is impossible to remember that they *are*, along with that supposed enemy in front of them, God's holy and beloved Child. The One Child of God is not complete without *all* of the perceived "enemies" upon the earth, and this is a painful existence when one is not able to remember the Truth of themselves, as well as the one in front of them.

If each one is seeking the remembering of their Oneness with each other and their relationship to God, this is not something that can happen in an instant and then be let go. It is something that must become a way of life, something that must be lived out every day, ultimately in every moment, so that you have the satisfaction, the fulfillment, and the Oneness that you are.

When one begins to remember who they really are and begins to see that Truth in the one in front of them, their whole perspective of the world and its purpose changes. The Holy Spirit is there for you in every moment, at every turn, at every stop and start; and It desires nothing more than to join with you, guide you, direct you, and translate for you so that you may be on your true path Home.

USING YOUR INNER VOICE

Candace: When I arrived in Silicon Valley to be with DavidPaul, it was the height of the Internet boom. I was not prepared for the pace of life and the different priorities and values there. Everyone I knew in Hawaii was on a spiritual path and wanted a deeper awareness and understanding of Truth; they knew about the work I did with the Holy Spirit and welcomed the opportunity to connect with this Voice through me. In Silicon Valley, the priority was stock options, and the few people who received sessions with the Holy Spirit would ask questions about their stock options.

Rarely sharing this Voice with others or listening on my own, I soon grew depressed and was guided to check in with this Voice each morning before beginning my day. I wrote down the communications I received and tried to apply them, but with so much going on in my life—leaving my Hawaiian paradise, losing my support system and friends, ending a three year relationship and beginning a new one—I wasn't very successful. Without being able to *apply* these messages, they were only helpful in the moments that I listened and remembered, which had become fewer and fewer as time went on.

Struggling with so much, my relationship with DavidPaul became strained. I began to lose my sense of purpose with this Voice, and before long, I was feeling very lonely and disheartened. In spite of these challenges, DavidPaul and I were determined to lead a guided life and do our best to do what was in our highest good, rather than what was easiest. Because of that, we decided to check in with this Voice every Sunday, which we called "church," and usually one time during the week as well. We asked questions about our relationship and sought guidance on seeing the best in one another. Through this ongoing connection with this inner guidance, we were able to work through these difficult times and eventually we became engaged.

For a while, life was wonderful. We spent much of our time planning our wedding and enjoying all that that entails, but after the honeymoon was over, our Silicon Valley life was back to normal. While we continued to "check in" every week, we did it with the desire to receive answers, rather than with the intention to experience our connection with God. For me, this took a lot of the meaning out of the relationship and didn't feed me the way I needed it to, although I didn't realize this at the time.

At some point, it seemed to me that life in Silicon Valley was not conducive to focusing on God. This was not true, but it was what I came to believe while living there. As a result, I resigned myself to feeling less alive and less connected to God and this Voice within me. When our daughter, Hannah, was born a couple of years later, she was all I needed to nearly forget about this Voice within me altogether.

Hannah was a very high maintenance baby and demanded all the attention and energy I had to give, and I gave it to her. Two years quickly passed. Then I stopped nursing her and woke up one day with the remembrance that I wanted a more meaningful internal life. I adored my daughter and I loved being her mother, but I also needed more of a connection with God, not to mention more of a connection with myself.

Around this time, DavidPaul and I were guided to write our family prayer, which would lead us in the direction of our true path. (See page 123 for our family prayer) Once we wrote our prayer, we were guided to say it over and over again throughout the day as if it were already true. As a result, I began to believe our prayer and my life began to unfold toward the intention of that prayer. I soon began to meditate again, and before long, I was checking in more often and had reestablished my relationship with this Voice within me. I felt happier and more connected with Truth than I had in a long time.

Eventually, we were guided to move to Oregon. DavidPaul and I had the same dream for as long as we could remember. We wanted to write a book that inspired and instructed people in how to hear God's Voice. The Holy Spirit had told me since the beginning to walk my talk so that when this book was written, it would be as truthful and applicable as possible. In the process of moving, I realized that a window had opened up for us to write this book. The only problem was ... I was still learning to walk my talk.

Like all relationships, my relationship with God has had its ups and downs, though in this case, it was painfully clear that all of these ups and downs were my doing. Once we landed in Oregon, we enrolled our daughter in preschool part time and began to focus our energy and attention on meditation and joining with God. We spent our time connecting with God's Voice and seeking guidance for the book. In the course of receiving communication, I learned and remembered so much Truth that my concepts about DavidPaul, God, and the world began to change radically.

For so long, I thought that hearing God's Voice was the goal, but in writing this book and in looking back on my struggles over the past twelve years, I now realize that hearing this Voice is only the first step. Beyond that, I needed to learn how to *use* this Inner Voice to guide my thoughts, my perceptions, my emotions, and therefore, my reality, so that I can live a happy, fulfilling life and move in the direction of Oneness with God and God's Child. I've come to see that having this inner Guide and Teacher is like having the right exercise machine. It's a great tool and it works, if I use it. If I don't, it just sits in the corner collecting dust, or its function changes and it becomes something to hang things on.

Even though I can hear God's Voice, I still have so much to learn about how to apply this Voice to my life. My gift is sharing this Voice. My life lesson is learning how to use It—a lesson I have been resisting for many years. I am now slowly

When one begins to remember who they really are and begins to see that Truth in the one in front of them, their whole perspective of the world and its purpose changes.

relearning how to experience that wonderful Presence in my mind Who makes loving observations wherever I go. I am realizing that there is only one True Voice in the world, and any others that I perceive, I made up. I am remembering that God's Voice is part of me and can guide me in all that I think and do in ways that can bring me unlimited peace.

I've often heard that people teach what they most need to learn, and this is certainly the case for me. My goal is to one day hear only God's Voice, and as this Voice for Love has said before, "that is not a matter of if, but when. The outcome is assured."

SHARING YOUR INNER VOICE

DavidPaul: Hearing and sharing God's Voice in the world can happen anywhere at anytime. It does not matter if you're in an important meeting, on the subway, riding a bike, sitting in traffic, working out at the gym, or waiting tables. It is possible to connect with Truth and hear the Voice for Truth in all that we do in life. This is why accessing our Inner Voice does not mean that we have to change our lives, become different people, or give up that which we love. It simply means to connect with God in our daily lives, to see the world through Eyes of Love, and to hear God's loving messages so that we may be filled with peace, acceptance, and understanding. In so doing, we bring Heaven into the world, into our families, our companies, and into everything we do.

We each have our own purpose for hearing and sharing this Voice for Love in our lives. Discovering this purpose may be simple for some or a process for others. In the first five years of hearing God's Voice as a recognizable voice within me, I never once shared this Voice with anyone else except Candace. Just the thought of sharing It with someone else was terrifying. Candace, on the other hand, started sharing this Voice with others her very first week of hearing It. While I felt confident that I could tune-in to this Voice whenever I wanted, sharing It aloud with another person was just too much for me to deal with. So I never tried.

One day several years ago, I was feeling really disappointed with myself for not being willing to share God's Voice with others, so I sat down to get some comfort and guidance, and this is what I heard:

Everyone has a different function and a different job. Everyone chose their job and their function, and being the introvert that you are, you have a very strong need to have your own sense of personal peace on a moment-to-moment, hour-to-hour, day-to-day basis. When you look at Candace, you see that her discipline and her struggles and challenges do not involve choosing peace on a consistent basis—certainly sometimes, and certainly eventually—but the desire for peace is not there at the moment of awareness of pain.

What you signed up for with this Voice was to have your own personal, real, obvious, and blatant connection so that you would have this resource for peace within you. That is the service you signed up for with the Holy Spirit. Do not think that Candace's is a "higher service" or anything like that because she can share these words with other people in this way. When you use God's Voice for its true intention, for its true function, to serve you in experiencing peace, to shift your perspectives to Truth, and to remember your Oneness with God, *that is it*. Then you *live* that, and you become a walking demonstration of that. That's what you signed up for. You have watched this one and witnessed what she has signed up for and that is not what you were interested in, is that true?

DavidPaul: In what ways? I wouldn't mind sharing this Voice with people.

Even if you did not choose having your own peace?

DavidPaul: No. I would rather have my peace than be able to share God's Voice with people.

And coincidentally, that's what you have. You got exactly what you wanted and what you signed up for. Candace, being an extrovert, a talker, social, more external, signed up for sharing God's Words, does a good job at it, and does not always choose peace at the awareness of pain. That's not to say that one is right or wrong, but it's also not to say that one is a higher calling. They are just different. By the nature of each personality, they serve God differently. Truly, by the nature of your essence, you have a certain path you go on.

You have a wonderful gift of the desire to seek and to choose peace and to use God's Voice in that way. Candace has the ability to share communication with other people, while your strength currently lies in experiencing your own peace in times of trouble, and your Oneness with God when you are feeling separate.

There are so many different ways for people to use this Voice within them to fulfill their purpose in life. Yours is more intimate and more personal. Candace's is more outward, and she offers that to everyone. It is not to try to imitate what Candace is demonstrating but to find your own groove, your own rhythm, and your own connection in relationship with God's Voice.

What you have can only be what you have chosen, and there is a part of you that is very aware that this is exactly as you would like it to be. You have a very strong desire to be of service and you have the belief that this is a way of being of service that you feel would work for you. You could say, "I share the Voice of God with people and that is my service," and yet, you have to contemplate what service really is. Is it what one lives and how they think, how they use their mind, or is it what one says out loud? So reshape or reframe for yourself what kind of service you would like to do. Would you rather have your peace in this moment or share God's Words with someone else? It is very obvious to you what you would choose. This is not to say you can only have one. That is not the point. The point is that *in this moment*, peace is what you are choosing.

You have a desire to use God's Voice in the way that your mate does because you have witnessed that sharing, have gained so much from it, and have seen others gain from it. You desire to have that too, and yet it is not your function right now. That can be disappointing or frustrating at times, and yet you would not compromise what you have with this Voice for anything. You desire to use this Voice to gain peace, insight, and a shift in perspective more than being of service, with your beliefs of what being of service is. As you utilize God's Voice in this way more and more, live the truths that you hear, and seek peace more frequently, you are living in the world in such a way that that *is* your service. Just holding the belief and the Reality of God's Voice and what this Voice can offer you *is* your service. Whether or not you share those words with others has nothing to do with it.

Candace experiences peace in sharing the words, and there can be more benefit for her in sharing the words with others and hearing the message that way than in seeking peace directly and getting an answer just for her. She often gets her answers through receiving answers for other people.

Others may fulfill their function and utilize their relationship with this Voice for Love within them in the way that they create a marriage, a family, a business, an organization that supports children or women in Afghanistan, or someone who writes music or songs of Truth, and so on. So many people are manifesting their relationship with God on earth whether it's conscious or not. Often times, they just don't discuss that part of their lives with others.

DavidPaul: Hearing this message brought me a lot of peace and self acceptance. I sat with it for many months and continued to take it in. Then one day, I took a long hike through the mountains to talk with God. It was a beautiful summer day, and I walked many hours in conversation with Him. As I approached my car at the end of the trail, my cell phone suddenly rang. A close friend was calling to ask for communication. Candace had always been the one to share God's Voice with him, but he had already called Candace at home and was unable to get in touch with her. He knew that I heard God's Voice as well, but he did not know that I had never shared this Voice with anyone. Feeling desperate for communication, he asked if I would be willing share God's Voice with him right then and there on the phone.

Although a wave of fear came over me when he asked, I was feeling really connected from the hike, so without giving it much thought, I said, "Ok. Let's do it."

Sitting in my car with my cell phone in hand, I closed my eyes and prayed to be able to share God's Voice with this person. After a few minutes of silence, I opened my mouth and started speaking. About 40 minutes and a slew of questions later, I hung up the phone feeling excited and happy to have shared God's Voice with someone besides Candace for the very first time. Ironically, I had just spent several months finally accepting the fact that sharing God's Voice in that way was *not* my life's path and would probably never happen!

Since that day, I have shared this Voice with hundreds of people and have come to experience ever more deeply that God's Voice truly *is* our Right-Mind. When I'm joined with this Voice, feeling this Presence of Love, and experiencing my Oneness with God's Voice as I share It, I truly experience that God's Voice *is* My Voice. In those moments, it's truly remarkable to experience communicating *to my Self as the Holy Spirit*. I literally experience that I am God's Voice and the Child of God with whom I am speaking with over the phone.

As a result of sharing God's Voice with others in this way, I now recognize and feel this Presence of Love in so many more areas of my life, and I have now come to see that sharing God's Voice is much more than sharing words with another person. It's truly about extending God's Love wherever we are, in whatever we're doing. Regardless of what it might look like, when we extend God's Love, we are fulfilling our purpose in the world. The form doesn't matter. The expression doesn't matter. It's the Content that matters. And the Truth is ... the Content is always there. We just have to choose to see It.

Fulfilling our purpose then is not about doing. It's about *being*. It's not about form or expression. It's about perception and the choosing of it. When we are in our Right-Mind, we recognize that we *are* fulfilling our purpose in that moment. To the ego, fulfilling our life's purpose requires that we *do* some thing in the world. In Truth, there is nothing that we need to do to fulfill our life's purpose. There is just the remembrance that we *are*. God *is*. I *am*. In that remembrance, we extend the Love that God *is* through form. In that now moment, we *are* the expression of God ... concerned not with the expression, but abiding in the eternal Presence of Love that *is* the expression unfolding and extending through us, within us, and as us in the world.

In that experience of being One with God, you have the perfect freedom, *as God*, to extend Love in whatever way you choose. Your will and God's Will are One. There are no rules, no expectations, no right or wrong. There is only God. And you, as God and as the Presence of Love, are free to extend your Self in whatever way your Heart desires.

When one has their own true religion, which is just to say their own true relationship with God that is lived out in the world, there is the consistent remembering of who they really are, which begins to become more of a belief than a theory.

UNCOVERING YOUR LIFE'S PURPOSE

DavidPaul: You said earlier that the meaning and purpose of life was to remember the Truth of who we are. Are you saying that *everyone* has the *same* purpose in life?

Yes, everyone has the same purpose in the world—the purpose of remembering their True Nature, remembering that they *are* pure Spirit, that they are not the forms they identify with in the world but the *Essence* from which all form arises. That is the One Purpose that is within all of God's Children, because that is the Purpose of this One Voice for Truth within you. That is the Purpose of the Holy Spirit; therefore, it is your Purpose as well, since your Mind is One.

How one goes about doing that is up to them. You have been given the free will to awaken in whatever way you choose. You, as the extension of God's Love, have the freedom to extend your Love in all the ways that are possible. God is indeed doing exactly that through you, right now, and in each and every moment. That is why each one has a different expression of being God in the world.

When one looks around in the world and sees how another is fulfilling their purpose, how another is extending their love and gifts in the world, it is common for that one to identify with the other's form or expression and then think that because that particular expression is so beautiful, so loving, and has such a wonderful impact, that somehow that person's purpose must be grander, more special, or that they are somehow more aligned with the Divine Plan than they are. When one is perceiving another in that way, they are missing what is truly happening. They are seeing the expression and forgetting its Source. They are seeing the form and missing the Essence that is being expressed and shared.

Your purpose in the world is to remember the Love that

you are and to share It. The form does not matter. There is no such thing as a grander expression of Love in the world. All Love expressed is equal. There is only God. Therefore, there is only Love being shared and expressed through all things and as all things. The expression or the form cannot increase or decrease the Love that is extended. All Love that is shared is given to all, for there is only One to extend It to.

When one is extending Love and Truth in the world, it does not matter whether they are extending a smile to the one in front of them, sitting on top of a mountain feeling the love they are and recognizing that love all around them, leading a company and bringing their love to that experience, or guiding their family through the day. Each and every one is experiencing the Love that they are and sharing that Love in whatever form it takes. The forms will come and go. The expressions will come and go—they are not eternal.

What is of true value and is everlasting are all of the moments that you *experience* Truth, the moments that you *feel* the Love that you *are* and share that love with the rest of your Self—be it a tree, a pet, your family, or an entire company— it does not matter. That is what is eternal. That is what stays within the Mind of God—forever.

No expression or form lasts forever. They will come and they will go as surely as the sun will rise and set, and yet the experience of Love that you bring to life is what remains. That is what grows and builds within the Mind of God. That is the extension of God that is rippling through all of Creation. That is your true purpose in the world—to *be* this Presence of Love in whatever form it takes.

But how do you know which form or expression is yours? Many want to know what their mission and purpose is. They might understand that their purpose is to extend Love and to be that Presence in the world, but because they identify with form, they have the belief that there must be a specific form or expression for them.

The Truth is ... it does not matter what the form is. Yes, there is a specific expression within you that is yearning to come out and be expressed, and certainly this Voice within you can help you discover and feel that within you, but in the end, you will come to realize that whatever you are guided to do by God, will in fact be what *you* desire, what is in *your* heart, where your passion and true interests lie, and where your dreams arise from. These things *are* the Voice for God within you—the expression of God within you wanting to burst through into the world to share all that you have with all that you are.

Yes, ask this Voice within you to help you discover these dreams and passions, and at the same time, *feel* what it is you truly want to do in the world. *Feel* the passion and the joy and the dreams that you have within you that come from this *state of being* that you *are*. When you do, fulfilling your purpose in the world will be certain. You will not be attached to the forms and expressions that come to you and through you to live out in the world, for you will abide in the *state of being* from which they arise. You will not be attached to what those forms and expressions look like as they flow through as your own desires, as your own passion, and as your own dreams, because your passions and your dreams for peace and love are, indeed, God's. You will come to experience that there is no separation between your Heart's desire and what God Wills for you. You will come to experience your union with God so fully that you will know that all that you desire to do is God's Will for you.

When one is in their Right-Mind, everything that comes to them—every inspiration, every thought, every desire, every inclination—is recognized as a thought from God. When one is in their Right-Mind, they experience their Self *as God* in the world.

So if you want to know what your purpose is in the world, remember the Truth of who you are. Join with this Voice for Love that you are. And when you become immersed in this Reality, you will know that every thought that arises within you—regardless of what it looks like, whether it's about your company, your family, your home office, or the people all around you—you will know that it is indeed the expression of God in the world, extending God's Love *as you* to all of Creation, and that you *are fulfilling* your purpose in the world by being that expression of Love, sharing that expression of Love, and awakening that Presence of Love in the rest of your Self—all 7 billion parts of You.

FULFILLING YOUR LIFE'S PURPOSE

DavidPaul: Being in relationship with Candace has been my greatest gift and my greatest challenge, and it's what has ultimately motivated me to discover my true religion. The first week Candace arrived from Hawaii to be with me, we went to Magic Mountain, an amusement park in Southern California, to celebrate. Although we had never exchanged a single kiss before her arrival, we loved each other deeply and were feeling incredibly alive and joyful at the thought of starting a life and a family together.

While eating lunch on the grass that day at Magic Mountain, we decided to go within and ask the Holy Spirit for a message. The message we received was about the magic of our union, why we were together, and the incredible gifts and rewards awaiting us in our future. But before we opened our eyes, the Voice said one thing that remains etched in my mind to this day. It told us that our union with one another would be quite a roller coaster ride, that we would have breathtaking highs and heart-wrenching lows and both would be part of the ride.

Afterward, we held hands and looked into each other's eyes. Filled with excitement and hope for our future together, we talked about the challenges God forewarned us about and made a commitment to see one another through God's Eyes in times of struggle and pain. I thought that my love for Candace was so strong and my understanding of Truth so unshakable that choosing Right-Mindedness would be an easy commitment to make.

Nine years have passed since that day at Magic Mountain. While I love Candace with all my heart and am so grateful for our life together, I humbly admit that our union has been the scariest, most challenging ride of my life. I have zoomed higher than I ever dreamed I would, but I have also plunged lower than I ever imagined I could—over and over and over again. I thought that my desire for peace, my understanding of Truth, and my know-how for choosing Love was enough, but I have continued to find myself saying and doing things I don't enjoy or prefer.

When Candace and I first sat down to work on this final chapter, we received a lot of personal communication about living our true religion more fully. At first, I didn't understand why we were talking about it so much. Then one day, Candace and I got into a really big fight, and I said some things that I wished I hadn't. When I stormed back to my office to calm down, a wave of melancholy came over me. I felt incredibly hopeless and sad for being so reactive and for not dealing with my thoughts and emotions more constructively, yet again for what seemed like the ten thousandth time. As I slumped on the couch in defeat, I closed my eyes and connected with God.

"What could I possibly do to stop myself from reacting this way?" I asked despairingly.

To my surprise, after more than an hour of talking with God, the answer I walked away with was "living my true religion." What unfolded during that hour was a dialogue that taught me the power of using a single, repeatable process for choosing peace in any situation. What I currently had was a hodgepodge of perspectives, goals, and techniques that I had collected over the past twelve years and used haphazardly. Through my conversation, I came to understand how knowing my true religion and developing a simplified approach to living it could support me in manifesting my heart's desire and fulfilling my purpose in the world. This was an incredible revelation for me.

The following week, I went within to learn how to put my true religion into practice.

Indeed, we have been waiting for this day, patiently and lovingly, knowing that this would truly be a moment of bringing this Voice into the world in such a way as to inspire you to truly *live* with this Voice. Thank you for wanting to more fully live the Truth of who you are in the world so that you know in every moment that what you are thinking and saying and doing is indeed that which is in your highest good. To know this in every moment is to experience your union with God. That is ultimately what you are seeking in your life and in your desire to determine how to live your true religion.

For you, your true religion is peace. It is what you came here to deepen. It is what you entered the world to more fully experience, and it is what you have come here to share with others. For you, peace is knowing the Truth of who you are, experiencing that Truth in your heart and mind, and sharing that Truth with all who truly want that for themselves, sharing that Truth with all who ask for it and who are open and willing to receive it—that is your true definition of peace, the definition you seek in your heart and mind to experience and live out in the world. So how then shall we experience this more fully in your wakeful life?

DavidPaul: God and I then spent the better part of an hour discussing what this might look like. We also created a simple process to help me experience peace more consistently, one that I could apply in any situation. While I was told that this process would continue to unfold over time, I am now using it in my daily life. While I don't expect my life to change overnight, nor do I believe I will always choose peace instead of pain from here on out, I feel very hopeful and excited to be applying it to my life, and I look forward to seeing where living my true religion takes me.

✧ EXERCISE – LIVING YOUR HEART'S DESIRE

Sit with a pencil and paper and write down all of the things that matter the most to you. This might be a way of feeling, being, doing, or seeing, rather than a favorite television show or your pet. Write down that which is most important to you that gives you satisfaction, fulfillment, joy, peace, or comfort. This might be something like loyalty, honesty, caring, or acceptance.

Then ask yourself, "What are my ultimate goals? How do I truly want to live?" Do you want to love your neighbor? Do you want to extend kindness wherever you go? Do you want to turn the other cheek? Do you want to see God in everyone you meet? Do you want to hear God's Voice? Do you want to be restored to your Oneness? Whatever it may be, think about what your ultimate goals are. List them and prioritize them so that you can discover *for you*, what is truly most important.

With that information, begin to contemplate how you could live that would incorporate all that matters to you. Spend some time in prayer with this list. Share your list with God. Spend some time in meditation with this list. Share it with the Holy Spirit. Ask for whatever guidance or direction can be given to you that you may come to understand how it is that you would like to live. Allow this guidance and direction to come in any form it may. You might perceive an answer while driving down the road, or when you wake from a dream, or after an encounter with another person. You may hear communication. You may get an insight or an inspiration. However it comes, begin to gather the pieces of guidance and direction that come to you. This may take days or weeks or longer.

As you gather together all of these pieces, you may want to make notes about the guidance and direction you receive and begin to establish a framework for how you want to live in the world so that your life unfolds in a way that brings you peace, joy, and comfort, and leads you in the direction of your highest goals. You might ask yourself in a challenging situation, "What would I do or how would I act if I were the person I want to be?" You will get an answer in one form or another about what to say, do, or think that supports you in that which matters the most to you. When you stop and ask yourself, "How is it that I can be who I dream of being?" and you receive some insight or direction and you follow through with that, then you *are* doing and being that which is your highest goal. It is not something that is out in the future, seemingly unattainable, or too lofty to even imagine. It is something that you are doing and being right now because you have determined what it is, how to get there, and are questioning yourself as you go along to keep you in line with your goal.

If you want to be a certain person one day, why not this day? Now that you know what that is and how to get there, it is very simple. This is what one could call their true religion. It is what they believe in, what matters to them, who they want to be, how they want to live in the world, how they want to interact with another, and how they want to perceive. It is *their* true religion, which has nothing to do with anyone else. It is only between you and God, and it affords you a way of living and perceiving in the world that enriches you in all the ways that truly matter to you.

CHAPTER SUMMARY

We all have the same purpose in life—to remember the Truth of who we are. How you go about fulfilling that purpose is up to you. God does not have any rules or expectations for how you go about that. There is only freedom, and you are free to choose whatever you want—whatever your Heart desires.

Accessing you Inner Voice to discover what you value and how you truly want to live is a sure path to fulfilling your purpose in the world. As you remember your true Identity and Oneness with God and reclaim your Power to be God's Love in form and expression, you become free to follow your Heart in every moment. You become free to live your highest vision for your Self in every moment ... knowing that what you do and how you do it *is* the extension of God's Love in the world.

Take the time to connect with this Voice for Love that you are. Take the time to discover your true religion. If you do, you *will*, without a doubt, come to live the life of your dreams and fulfill your true purpose in the world.

About the Authors

DavidPaul Doyle and Candace Doyle are the founders of The Voice for Love, a leading nonprofit organization and global community of people who join together in celebration to give and receive love, communication, inspiration, learning, and support for hearing God's Voice in their lives.

The Voice for Love's worldwide team of students and certified spiritual counselors, coaches, and teachers provides education and training through its free global telephone hotline, training and resource center, and through its many public events, including workshops, weekend intensives, tele-seminars, and certification programs throughout the world.

For more information and to get involved in this growing movement of true personal empowerment, visit www.thevoiceforlove.com or contact:

The Voice for Love
PO Box 3125
Ashland, OR 97520
541-488-0426
www.thevoiceforlove.com
love@thevoiceforlove.com

CPSIA information can be obtained at www.ICGtesting.com
Printed in the USA
BVOW05s1117010415

394286BV00004B/212/P